Effective Coaching

Effective Coaching

Teaching Young People Sports and Sportsmanship

Pat Cassidy

WESTHOLME
Yardley

Published by Westholme Publishing, LLC, Eight Harvey Avenue,
Yardley, Pennsylvania 19067
www.westholmepublishing.com

ISBN 1-59416-014-7

First Printing
0 9 8 7 6 5 4 3 2 1

Printed in the United States of America
on acid-free paper

To my wife, Jen, and our daughters, Erin and Megan, for allowing me the time and energy necessary to be the kind of coach I want and need to be, and to my Mom and Dad, my most important coaches

Contents

Preface

I became the varsity baseball coach at Broad Run High School in Ashburn, Virginia, when I was twenty-two years old. My coaching experience consisted of a year as a volunteer coach on the Broad Run baseball staff and two years of coaching the school's summer league basketball team. Coming straight from four years of college studying English and playing basketball at The Catholic University of America in Washington, D.C., I thought teaching and coaching seemed like the natural progression for someone who had spent his entire life as a student-athlete. But as much as I had studied to become a teacher, I was about to realize that I had no true education to prepare me to be a coach. When I got this opportunity at my high school alma mater, in a suburban area about thirty miles from Washington, D.C., I had no idea what I was getting myself into.

At the time I was feeling a mix of emotions. I was excited at the chance to run my own high school baseball program and was eager to start working with the players. My nervousness was probably due to the fact that I knew that I was in over my head. This was the first time in my life that I stepped onto an athletic field or court not knowing what to expect. The one thing that got me through the initial roller coaster of emotions in my first year was that I knew I would do everything in my power to make it a good season for my players and the team, and if that meant spending lots of hours and learning fast, that's what I intended to do.

When I began coaching there were very few resources to turn to outside of my own experience. This is not unusual. Nearly four million individuals in the United States coach youth athletics. Almost all of them are volunteers—parents, school teachers, former athletes, local park employees—and almost all of them begin coaching without any formal instruction. I was fortunate as a young head coach to have had a tremendous amount of help learning the ropes from those who had coached me in the past in Little League, high school, and college. And other coaches are, of course, some of the best teachers. But not everyone has this resource. When I started, I wished I had a written guide that explained some of the common pitfalls of coaching as well as productive tips and recommendations.

After more than a decade of coaching high school athletics, I decided to share some of my experiences that I hope will benefit those individuals who begin one of the most important and rewarding experiences in working with young people. I provide practical advice to someone new to coaching to help them handle the numerous situations a coach faces: how to communicate effectively with your athletes, your staff, and parents, planning practices, scheduling games or matches, acquiring assistant coaches, and fundraising, to name just a few. I am not an expert, but I am no longer a novice; I am at a point in my career where my missteps and achievements are still fresh in my mind and can serve as examples for others to consider. Although my players have experienced individual and team success, at times I have made common coaching mistakes and at other times I have stumbled onto a few things that turned out to be right; all of these are here. I was a certain type of coach in my first year, a different type of coach in my fifth year, and another kind of coach today, and I now finally feel that I have a good grasp on the fundamental aspects of being a head coach.

The purpose of this book is to help you in your own coaching—whether it's your son's Little League team, the winter basketball clinic at a local Y, or your daughter's soccer team—and to make the experience enjoyable for you and your players. Coaching at any level is hard work, and to do it well you have to have a passion for the sport and for teaching young people. I hope the ideas in this book will help you feel the same way I do about the tremendous opportunity and responsibility you have every time someone calls you "coach."

So Now You're a Coach: Some Fundamentals

They call it coaching, but it is teaching. You do not just tell them. . . you show them the reason why.—Vince Lombardi

You just volunteered to coach your daughter's youth league basketball team. You played in high school ages ago and still play pick-up games at your neighborhood recreational center. So coaching a group of thirteen eight-year-olds can't be that tough, right? Think again.

Whether your introduction to coaching is similar to this scenario, or if you are coaching the junior high football team because the principal told you that it was part of the physical education teaching job you just accepted, or if you are simply trying to get involved with neighborhood kids as a volunteer, you will soon find out that coaching today's young athletes means much more than assigning players to positions and calling a few plays.

Whether you are completely new to the profession, have a little coaching experience, or have coached at one level and plan to move up, there is something that binds each one of us who decides to coach: a basic desire to take your responsibilities of teaching others seriously, to improve your techniques—to be an effective coach. Effective coaches, at any level, have certain character traits in common. Regardless of whether they are coaching a recreational soccer team or a high school basketball squad, successful coaches are able to do more than make decisions on game day. The most important character traits of effective coaches are not whether they can teach a pitcher how to throw a curve ball or a football player how to tackle properly; what is crucial is their ability to understand and communicate with people: players, parents, other coaches, officials, or the media.

If a beginning coach asked me how to be an effective coach, I would offer the following three fundamental tips:

1. Understand the responsibility and value of working with young people.
2. Maintain a proper and realistic perspective about sports.
3. Always remember why you decided to coach in the first place.

These three guidelines help less-experienced coaches avoid some common beginners' mistakes and gain a healthy perspective on the responsibilities of coaching. Chapters 2 and 3, which outline effective principles for coaching, build on these three fundamentals of coaching. These apply to any team sport, especially those popular in youth leagues today: soccer, baseball, softball, basketball, football, hockey, and swimming.

1. Understand the responsibility and value of working with young people.

Effective coaches realize that playing sports is one step of many in a young person's life. One day in the future, your athletes will stop participating in competitive sports. Ultimately, the real world will ask these former players to show up for work, understand the value of cooperating with others, expect them to make sacrifices, and so on.

Young people who play for a responsible coach will likely learn these positive values or have them reinforced through athletics. Good coaches preach and demonstrate the value of a solid work ethic. It is a trait that will help a young football player on the gridiron; more importantly, it will serve that athlete well one day whether he decides to be a business owner, department store manager, or a doctor. A basketball coach teaches his players about the importance of playing team defense, which means learning to be able to work with others. Baseball coaches teach their players about the sacrifice bunt, where a player intentionally makes an out to advance a teammate on the bases—

another valuable lesson in teamwork and coopera-
tion. But using one's time and energy to help others may be the most important thing an effective
coach can teach athletes.

Ultimately, every coach must sooner or later
wonder, "What have I taught these athletes that
will benefit them when they stop playing sports
(at age fifteen, eighteen, or twenty-three)?" If the
only thing my players remember about playing
basketball or baseball ten years after they are out
of high school is how to attack a zone defense or
how to protect the plate with two strikes, then I
have failed. Much more significant in the long
run is teaching players real-life lessons that will
help them become better people when they become
the next generation of workers, parents, and
coaches.

As much as a coach might want to focus on
turning kids into winners on the athletic field, it
is equally important to focus on their development
as people. Using in-your-face tactics or intimida-
tion to motivate a ten-year old will do much more
damage than good. As athletes enter their teens
and the stakes involved with athletics start to
grow, then a coach may begin to raise his expectations for effort and desired results from his players. Ultimately, a coach must understand that he
must treat certain aspects of coaching ten-year
olds very differently from a thirteen- or eighteen-
year old athlete. Their physical and mental capa-
bilities are vastly different, and the coaching strategy needs to reflect this.

2. Maintain a proper and realistic perspective about sports.

One of the most important traits of an effective coach is to maintain a proper perspective on the roles of sports in the big picture. Many persons enter coaching right after college, while others are parent volunteers whose sports associations are based on their high school or college playing days. In both cases, passion for sports and competition are often strong, perhaps too strong, and learning how to redirect these emotions is among the first steps to becoming an effective coach.

My view on the role of sports and competition in life has changed completely since I was a rookie coach feeling my way through things. As a novice coach, I made numerous mistakes in the way I ran my program. I made excessive demands of my coaching staff, my players, and myself. During practices and games, I focused my attention on trying to catch my players making a blunder so I could yell that they were doing it wrong, instead of using positive reinforcement by observing and letting my players and teams know what they were doing right. Although I was coaching students who chose to play sports, even volunteer coaches in T-ball, soccer, and other sports in recreational leagues can face this pitfall.

Another mistake I made early on was living and dying with every basket on the hoop court and every run scored on the baseball diamond. I

overcoached by constantly telling my teams nearly every positive or negative thought that crossed
my mind. This made some of my players nervous
and on edge. I had players who were scared to
make a mistake, instead of taking a risk and trying to make a great play to help our team.

But the worst thing that I did as a young
coach was to react poorly to losing. During the
first few years, when my teams would lose a game
I figured we lost for one of two reasons: either my
players were not playing hard enough or they
were not listening to me. So, like many young
coaches, I would yell louder or make my team go
through longer, more difficult practices. I figured
that if the players saw how miserable losing made
me, and if they realized how much they would
hate my postgame speech and the next day's practice when we lost, they would surely improve their
play. I told my players to keep things in perspective, but I did not do this myself. What kind of lesson was I teaching these kids?

What made me a better coach was learning to
have a more realistic, balanced view of the importance of sports in the grand scheme of life. As rare
as it is that a player goes on to have professional
success in sports, it is unlikely that any coach will
go on to the national level. "There are more important things in life" is a cliché, but it is hard for most
people to have perspective about something they
are passionate about, particularly young people.

It would be nice if a coach could learn to put

sports into perspective simply by saying that they will. But we all know it isn't that easy. For me, there was the natural march of time. As a head coach in my early twenties, I simply was not willing to look in the mirror and tell myself that I was not doing as good a job as I thought I was with my players, or that my team may have needed a different leadership style to be successful. Sports also consumed my every waking moment. When my team would struggle on the field or court, I would come home and overanalyze every videotape, every statistical sheet, and every practice plan to see what my players and I should be doing differently. Now, more than ten years later, I've become a more mature person. I have a family, and I can't wait to get home to spend time with them. I am more relaxed and I think more clearly when I am coaching my players the day following a big win or a tough loss.

Experiences can also help a coach achieve a healthy perspective on sports. One year my team lost a baseball playoff game on what appeared to be a questionable call by an umpire. I was not happy with the umpire, and neither were my players or their parents. The next day at school, I was about to tell one of our assistant principals about how devastating this loss was to our program, when we were interrupted by our principal, who told us there was an emergency and we had to evacuate students from an area of our school immediately. Later in the day, when things were

A coach is one of the most important role models in a young athlete's life. (Bob Updegrove)

back to normal, the assistant principal came by my room and asked for me to finish my story. I told him that it was just a game. And despite everyone's disappointment with the officiating, I had to remember that referees and umpires are often volunteers and just as inexperienced as the coaches, particularly in recreational sports. It's not worth getting so mad and frustrated that it clouds your own good judgment.

I dwell on this not just for the benefit of you, the coach. Your players, whether they are six years old or sixteen years old, watch your actions and pick up clues about how they should behave. Effective coaches know not to treat athletic contests as life-or-death situations. A good basketball coach doesn't scream at an official or walk on the court every time a call goes against her team.

Reasonable baseball coaches don't tear into their pitcher if he happens to unintentionally walk an opposing batter. Seasoned soccer coaches don't tell their players that scoring a goal is the most important thing they will do in their life. Sports are games. Successful coaches show their players how to remain positive and try to help players overcome difficulties they face on and off the courts and athletic fields. A responsible coach does everything in his power to teach his players to put forth their best effort, to respect others, and to handle losing—and winning—with class.

3. Always remember why you decided to coach in the first place.

Effective coaches remember why they began coaching, whether it was a week ago or fifteen years ago. In many cases, playing sports or playing for a particular coach inspired them to get involved in helping young people themselves. Most coaches at schools are former athletes who experienced great success in their younger days. Other coaches are parents whose children have expressed an interest in sports and in order to field a team in a local league, they volunteer to be a coach. All of these coaches took the step to share their expertise with athletes or find satisfaction in their role as a mentor.

I coach because I know from my years as an athlete the tremendous impact that playing sports and learning from coaches can have on an individual. At every level of my involvement in sports—from playing on a state championship baseball team in high school to being captain of a successful basketball team in college—I had the opportunity to play for dedicated coaches who were as concerned about instilling sportsmanship and the love of the game as building specific skills. And it is this dedication to developing young people through sports that is one of my primary motivations for coaching. I am sure that the same can be said for most of you who reflect on your own experience playing sports in school or in local leagues. But is this reflection alone a good indication about whether or not you really want to become a coach?

It is important to keep in mind that coaching is, in many ways, more challenging than playing. As a player you have the opportunity to physically control the outcome of a contest: you can make the crucial shot, or hit in the go-ahead run. As a coach, you make decisions that may affect a game's outcome, but you cannot control the game's action. You make decisions that you hope will improve your team's chances for success, and the rest is up to your players (and a bit of luck).

If you played on a lot of winning teams in your own athletic experience and you're thinking about coaching, ask yourself several questions. Will you love coaching if your team loses a lot of games? Will you be eager to come to practice each day if your team has little or no talent? Likewise, if you decide to volunteer to be a coach, will you have the patience and time to commit to these children every practice? If you can honestly answer "Yes" to these tough questions, then you have the right attitude to coach young people effectively.

My teams' levels of success and personal coaching experiences have been more varied than I ever imagined. I have had a team finish a season with fifteen wins and I have been voted district coach of the year. I have also had a team lose most of its games and wondered if I would still have a job at the end of the season. Regardless of the many ups and downs of coaching, I still enjoy teaching young players how to play the sports that I love.

It's now time to move on to some of the most important principles that guide all effective coaches.

2

Principles of Effective Coaching

Never quit. It is the easiest cop-out in the world. Set a goal and don't quit until you attain it. When you do attain it, set another goal, and don't quit until you reach it.
—Paul "Bear" Bryant

The first thing that any coach needs to know is that there is no single way to be successful with athletes at any level. A head coach can lead a team in one of many directions, but the majority of successful coaches have distilled their approach into clearly stated philosophies and goals for their athletes, game strategies that consistently prove successful for the team, and an understanding of how to get their players to go from being individuals to becoming a close-knit, focused team working toward common goals. Coaches who don't have clear goals, strategies, or a coaching philosophy are often questioned by players and their parents about their ability to lead a team; the results of this type of coaching can include confusion and frustration all around—and take the focus off the most important goal: teaching young people sports and sportsmanship.

The following principles are the key ideas and recommendations that most successful coaches employ and that all coaches should become familiar with, both those who are just starting out and those with coaching experience. Some may seem obvious, but it is surprising how few coaches actually follow even the most basic principles. I compiled these principles from coaches that I have played for, played against, coached with, and observed on the sideline, and from my own growth as a head coach. These principles are not a guaranteed recipe for success, but by examining and implementing one or more of them, you may improve your own team's competitive edge and create a more rewarding coaching experience for you and your players. At the very least, they will provide answers and guidance about where to begin, how to accomplish certain tasks and goals, and what to do when faced with difficult problems. The principles in this chapter are intended for coaches at all levels and for all sports; several additional principles are geared to older players or more elite sports programs and are discussed in the next chapter.

Notice that these principles say next to nothing about strategy, game plans, or winning, because great coaching is about larger issues. Sure, an athletically gifted team may trounce most of its opponents whether the coach is effective or not, but a well-coached team that makes its best effort whether they win or lose is just as successful as a team with lots of talent. Coaching is as much about how you work with the people around you and what you teach them as it is about developing and showcasing your or your athletes' talents.

Principles of Effective Coaching
Effective coaches . . .

1. Have a clearly stated philosophy about coaching and working with young people.

2. Have clearly stated priorities about how sports fit with other areas of an athlete's life.

3. Set realistic goals for themselves, their teams, and their athletes.

4. Are excellent communicators.

5. Are very well organized and have a strong work ethic.

6. Run purposeful, efficient practices.

7. Have the courage to make difficult decisions and are not afraid to admit mistakes.

8. Assess their team's strengths and weaknesses and play to the strengths.

9. Understand that their playing careers are over.

10. Are always looking to learn and improve as coaches.

11. Make playing sports fun for their athletes and have fun coaching.

Effective coaches have a clearly stated philosophy about coaching and working with young people.

Effective coaches make their philosophy about coaching clear to their staff members, players, and their players' parents. My coaching philosophy, for instance, starts with the idea that my staff members and I will do everything reasonable in our power to run a quality high school baseball program. That sounds pretty fundamental, but it is important to always keep this in mind because it is easier to forget than you might assume. A quality program means that our commitment and responsibility to the players as individuals has as much weight as figuring out how to achieve victories. Although we are all very competitive people, we do not believe in winning at all costs. We make sure our athletes know they will work hard, and we want them to have fun.

This overall philosophy is made clear to players and parents before the season starts through our preseason meeting for prospective players and through the "Meet the Coach Night" sponsored by our school's athletic department. By doing this, the coach helps all the parties involved with an athletic team avoid problems during the course of the season. I make sure my assistant coaches understand that we take our responsibility to our athletes very seriously. The various aspects of our program's philosophy are included in writing on the first page of each of my coach's playbooks:

"Run a quality, year-round baseball program"
• Including challenging games, well thought-out practices, weight lifting, optional winter workouts, team travel, team dinners, facility upgrades.

"Help players get into college"
• Including writing college letters of recommendation, calling college coaches to promote players, sending players to college showcases/camps.

"Make sure players know we care about more than baseball"
• Including communicating to players about non-baseball issues like school/grades, jobs, family or social issues.

The fact that each assistant coach and I have a written copy of this statement in our playbook helps to serve as a daily reminder as to what we are trying to teach and how we plan on doing it. A written coaching philosophy provides the framework on which to build your team.

To develop a coaching philosophy, you must ask yourself what you want to accomplish with your players and team. You must then determine the strategies and methods you will use to achieve your various goals. The philosophy of many coaches involves a statement about winning. There is nothing wrong with this if a coach states from day one that his main purpose of working with his players is teaching them to be successful in terms of wins and losses. Then everyone is on the same page. I have played for coaches like this; my teammates and I knew that our coach meant business and that he had high expectations about the desired results for our upcoming season.

It is also important for a coach to know who he is coaching and what expectations his athletes have about the sport. Organized junior high school and high school sports coaches should expect to be in competition to win. Although a youth league coach may want to win and want to have winning as part of his philosophy, he should realize that his philosophy must differ from that of a high school or AAU coach, who is working with older players and therefore can place a greater emphasis on winning and losing. The effective coach of very young athletes understands that he is coaching at a developmental level where winning and losing are parts of the game but that the principles of teamwork and good sportsmanship are paramount. An example of a youth league football coach's philosophy may look like:

Little Bears Football Coaching Philosophy
All Little Bears Football Coaches will . . .

• Work to help every player improve individually in his football skills.

• Teach players the values of teamwork and respect.

- Help the team improve in all three major areas (offense, defense, and special teams) each week of the season.
- Make every day of practice and games fun for all players.
- Speak with Little Bears about issues other than football (like school, issues at home).
- Teach our players to win with class.
- Teach our players to learn from adversity.

While similar in some aspects, the philosophy of a coach of a high school basketball program may look more like this:

Woods High School Warriors Basketball Program Philosophy

The Woods High School Basketball Staff will . . .

1. Run a quality, year-round basketball program including purposeful practices, games, summer leagues, camps, and weight training.

2. Teach players to set and follow priorities (Family/Academics/Basketball).

3. Maintain high standards for behavior and academic performance for all members of the basketball program.

4. Instruct players in basketball fundamentals in team and individual settings.

5. Attempt to help our players succeed in the classroom and on the basketball court.

6. Work year-round toward the goal of qualifying for the regional playoffs.

7. Communicate to every player that we are concerned with more than our players' athletic ability by discussing issues such as college plans, jobs, home life, etc.

8. Get involved in our community by running summer camps and inviting youth league teams and their coaches to practices and games.

9. Help promote players to college programs.

10. Build a program that the students, staff, and community will be proud to support year in and year out.

I want to make two points about the depth of this statement and the emphasis on winning. First, some coaches may feel that the range of ideas in the "Warriors Basketball Program Philosophy" is too broad and may feel that they would be overwhelmed by having so many areas to focus on. Your philosophy needs to be only as broad as you can comfortably handle. This also applies whether you happen to have a staff or you rely on parent volunteers. It is better to focus on a few areas and do them well, rather than to try to accomplish too many things and not be successful at any of them. Second, notice that the only time this particular coach's philosophy vaguely mentions winning is when he states the goal of qualifying for the regional playoffs. Some coaches may want to move this point up in the order of priorities in their philosophy, which is an individual call. Even though this statement does not mention winning, it does not mean that this coach fails in his responsibilities to his players to run a great athletic program. By stressing a year-round commitment, teaching priorities, academic success, promoting players to colleges, community involvement, and so on, this coach obviously has numerous ways to develop his players and his program. Winning games is just one of the ways to accomplish this goal. In most cases, coaches are not hired at the youth league or high school level based strictly on winning games; coaches are usually hired to teach young athletes how to play sports as part of an educational experience. The young players you coach are not paid to win, and in most cases, coaches are not judged solely on wins and losses. This is a point that effective coaches are able to keep in mind throughout the ups and downs of any season.

The last point I will make regarding developing your coaching philosophy is to be realistic. Don't be afraid to have high expectations for yourself, your staff, and your athletes, but always keep in mind the age level and talent of the athletes you are coaching. As a coach, you must be able to step back, look at each season, and determine whether your philosophy needs to be altered. It's a good idea to reassess your coaching approach before, during, and after a season. If the ideas you have about coaching change, so should your philosophy and how you work with your players. When I first started coaching baseball my philosophy was strictly about winning championships. Over the years, my philosophy has changed as I analyzed what was really important for the players and teams I coach. I no longer judge the efforts, sacrifices, and accomplishments of my players, teams, and coaching staff solely on winning championships. While we still strive every year to reach the postseason, I emphasize to my players, coaches, and parents that my primary goal is that the players in our program have a positive experience in a quality athletic program.

> The coach's overall philosophy of coaching needs to be made clear to players and parents before the season starts.

Effective coaches have clearly stated priorities about how sports fits with other areas of an athlete's life.

Effective coaches make sure that their players understand what is truly important. Usually this comes from identifying and teaching athletes a specific set of priorities. The priorities I teach my players come from Morgan Wooten, the legendary basketball coach of DeMatha High School in Hyattsville, Maryland. Coach Wooten listed the priorities he taught his players as follows: A)

Religion, B) Family, C) Academics, D) Basketball. Although he won over 1,000 games as a high school coach, nowhere does he mention winning basketball games.

I once heard Coach Wooten speak at a clinic and I remember him saying, "If you ever have problems at any point in your life, ask yourself if you are keeping your priorities in line. . . . If a student-athlete is more concerned about his jump shot than his History grade, he needs to check his priorities." His words encouraged me to understand that coaching and teaching young people should be about much more than winning and losing games. Coaching has much broader responsibilities than I ever imagined when I first stepped onto the field to lead a group of athletes.

At the top of my team rules is a list of priorities that all my players agree to abide by in order to participate in our baseball program. Family/religion are first, academics is second, and baseball is third. I combine Wooten's first two items, religion and family, into a large first priority, since I teach at a public school and religion is a personal issue. But my student-athletes know that whatever their religion or family situation, those are more important than their athletic commitments. After discussing the importance of priorities and rules in both the individual players' lives as well as our team's chances for success, I have the players sign the rules to acknowledge that they understand them and that they will do their best to follow these guidelines during the season. Having players sign team rules is essential to the process of teaching young people that they will be held accountable for their actions.

A set of priorities is beneficial at all levels of athletics. A Little League softball coach might teach her players what priorities she wishes to stress by using simpler language and goals when explaining to six- or seven-year-olds how to approach different aspects of their lives. The priorities she teaches might include:

- Be a good person.
- Try my best in everything I do.
- Listen to my parents, teachers, and coaches.

The coach of the Little League softball team may also want to discuss these priorities and team rules with the parents of young players who may not fully comprehend the guidelines for participating on her team. If a signature on the team rules is necessary, it may be best if the parents of each player sign them so that they can help their child understand the process of learning these values.

I make it part of my responsibility as a coach to emphasize academics with my student-athletes, and I collect report cards the day they come out. After all, in addition to being a coach, I am an English teacher. I do not demand straight-A work from my student-athletes, of course, but I stress the importance of turning in all assignments on time, completing homework, seeking out teachers for extra help, and so on. I also make it clear that if they can't show up for class on time, be respectful of classmates and teachers, apply themselves to their studies as best as they can, represent themselves and teammates in a positive fashion in the hallways, on bus rides, and so on, they won't play for me. Playing sports is not a right; it is a privilege. And it is important for athletes to understand that privileges can be taken away.

The fact of the matter is that most high school athletes' careers will end just there—in high school. The grades that student-athletes earn in the classroom and their scores on the SATs or other standardized tests will affect their lives in the long term, while the numbers they put up on the playing fields or courts will affect their popularity with their teammates and fellow students just in the few years they're in school. You have to ask yourself as a coach whether a student's GPA or their batting average matters more. Beyond high school, student-athletes must understand that if they are serious about participating in sports at the college level, then they must be dedicated to both their academic and athletic pursuits. If they choose to put all their time and energy into sports and fail to maintain their grades, then they will severely limit their options to participate in sports in college (even if they have the talent).

Teaching players where athletics fits alongside their other priorities (family, academics, etc.) helps young people develop personally and promotes sportsmanship.

Effective coaches set realistic goals for themselves, their teams, and their athletes.

The goals coaches set for themselves, their teams, and their athletes should vary depending on each team's strengths and weaknesses. With a team of experienced, talented players, earning a postseason berth or winning a certain postseason title may be realistic. With a young or inexperienced team, coaches will emphasize executing a certain number of quality pitches, plays, or possessions instead of focusing only on winning. With this outlook, a team that is overmatched night after night and loses consistently can take something positive away from what is sure to be a frustrating experience.

Teaching players to set realistic goals is another way that coaches can help their players improve individually, which in turn helps the team. For example, it wouldn't be a realistic or fair expectation for a softball coach to tell one of her returning players, "Jessie, I know you had a .148 batting average last year. This year, let's say that your goal is to hit .325. If you do that, we probably won't lose a game." Besides being unrealistic, this type of goal puts immense pressure on a player. A more realistic and fair approach to the athlete may go something like this, "Jessie, I know you struggled at the plate last year, but you finished up the last three games with five hits. Keep working as hard as you can. Let's set your offensive goal at a .280 batting average. I know you

Good coaches know how to help players achieve goals while keeping their athletes' priorities in order. (Glenn Shaup)

practiced your swing all off-season, so I know you can do it. If you and a few of your teammates each hit close to .300, we have a chance to win more games this year than last year." Setting a realistic goal and spreading the responsibility among Jessie and her teammates will take the pressure off one athlete.

With a very young team, goals may be as simple as each member of a T-ball team getting at least one base hit or scoring at least one run during the season. Individual goals might be to catch at least one fly ball. Setting realistic goals, even for very young teams, makes the activity more enjoyable for both the coach and the players.

I know that at times I have set the bar too high for certain players and teams. I have learned, however, to purposely set the goals for some players and teams a bit higher than I feel they have a reasonable chance to attain. By setting the goal somewhat higher than what I believe the player is capable of, I hope to keep him constantly working hard in an effort to improve. For example, if I am confident that a player who hit .275 as a sophomore on my varsity team has improved in the off-season through extra workouts to the point where he most likely will hit .305, I will sit down with him and set a goal of hitting .325 for the upcoming season. I will explain that I have confidence that his off-season workouts will result in a large increase in his batting average and this in turn will help to build up the player's confidence in his own ability. I set a high but realistic goal. By building up a player's confidence, an effective coach helps make reachable a goal that seemed unattainable a year before. It is important to note that coaches who do not set goals or who set goals too low often find that players underachieve and may feel satisfied by meeting a modest goal when they could be performing at an even higher level.

An effective coach also has to be prepared for a player or team not to achieve a goal. A coach must be willing to reassess the goals he sets during and after a season. If a high school baseball coach sets the goal of finishing in the top two places in the league standings, but his team gets off to a 2-8 start because of an inexperienced lineup, the coach should admit that he might have set his sights too high for his young squad. Therefore, at the halfway point in the season, he might say that his goal now is to have the team finish in the top five places in the league standings by winning five of the last ten contests. By setting realistic goals and reassessing those goals throughout the season, a coach is able to give his players and himself a clear idea of what they should be able to accomplish by season's end. And this sends the right signals to the players: that the coach is paying attention, understands the situation, and does not blame them for not achieving a goal.

Goals matter in each season, but it's also important for coaches to think ahead to a year or even five years from now. Effective coaches have an idea of how their team or program should grow in various stages. This vision does not necessarily have to involve a specific number of wins and losses. A coach's vision is normally tied in with the goals he sets for his team and program. For example, a football coach's preseason goal may be that he generates so much interest and excitement about his program that 100 athletes come out for the team. A midseason goal may involve a team's record, and end of the year goals could involve qualifying for postseason play or a certain number of his players earning all-conference honors. Long term goals may include making the playoffs a year from now for a very young team or for a school that is opening its doors for the first time with very few experienced athletes. Five years from now, a coach may determine that his program should be a playoff contender year in and year out.

A Little League baseball coach working with eight-year-olds may have an entirely different vision from that of a coach in a more competitive situation. If half of the players on his team are first-time baseball players, he may envision a team that is playing "fundamental baseball" consistently during the second half of the season. By having a longer term vision of his team playing consistently he allows his team (and himself) the time needed for improvement.

If a coach doesn't have realistic goals for his team or program, then he runs the risk of everyone (staff and players alike) to simply go through the motions with the attitude that sooner or later they will be successful (which is not always the case). Having a vision as to where the team should be at different points and times sets a timetable on what type of achievement will be acceptable for a staff and players and when it should happen. Achieving goals also promotes respect among the players for each other and for the coach.

Effective coaches are excellent communicators.

Coaches should be able to communicate clearly with their staff, athletes, and parents. Many coaches at all levels possess great amounts of knowledge about their various coaching disciplines, but being able to share their ideas with the players they coach is an entirely different issue. My high school baseball coach, Wayne Todd, gave me advice on communicating with athletes that I still use with my own players today. He explained to me that a good coach clearly discusses with an athlete both the positive and negative aspects of their performances. Athletes want to be told when they have done something right, and they need to be told when they have done something wrong.

One thing about coaches who communicate effectively is that they speak honestly with their players. The most misunderstood issue among players and coaches often revolves around playing time. Sometimes, players and coaches don't listen to what the other has to say regarding this issue. While the player has his ideas about what he may need to do to earn more playing time, a coach must clearly state his criteria for a player's game minutes to improve. A head coach who communicates directly, specifically, and honestly tells his athlete what he views as that player's strengths and weaknesses. For example, if a basketball player asks a coach why she is not getting more playing time, a coach can respond vaguely by saying, "I think the player ahead of you is playing a little better than you are right now." Compare this with the coach who says, "Even though your effort has been good, your free throw percentage is very low and your turnover to assist ratio is very high. If you work hard to improve in these two areas, you increase your chances of getting more playing time significantly." By responding specifically a coach can point out exactly where an athlete must improve for her playing time to increase. The head coach alleviates any misconceptions as to why the athlete is not getting as much playing time as she feels she deserves.

Coaches who are good communicators most often will start and end their practice with a brief set of comments to set the team's direction for the day or week. A football coach might start out practice letting his team know that they are going to place a special emphasis on punt coverage during that day's practice because that has been problematic for the team in recent games. This helps every member of the team to make a mental note that they are expected to improve in this area. At the end of practice, the coach may summarize where the team stands and what goals he has for the coming week. Or a baseball coach may remind his team that they have been doing a great job hitting the last few games, and that the team needs to win one of their upcoming three games left in the season to qualify for the postseason. This would leave players with an optimistic feeling about their recent play and reinforce their chances for extending their current season.

Good communication is necessary at all levels of play, particularly with very young or inexperienced athletes. An effective coach only gives his team as much information as they are capable of handling. The coach of a five-year-olds' soccer team may tell her team at the beginning of practice that today practice will focus on using both the right foot and left foot when dribbling the ball so their opponent cannot take the ball away from them. For five-year-olds, this is probably more than enough information for them to digest. At the end of practice, the coach may ask players if they feel like they have improved at dribbling the ball using both feet. More importantly, she should ask her young players if they had fun. As a coach, hopefully you hear the answer, "Yes," to both questions. The point I am making is that coaches have to be careful about how much information they give to young athletes at one time. If you use terminology that is too complicated or if you move too fast, you'll most likely only frustrate your athletes, and ultimately, yourself.

Coaches also must make sure the individuals on their team each have a clear understanding of their role on the team. On a basketball team, not everyone is going to be the go-to person who takes twenty shots per game, but a good coach makes sure that all players know they are valuable to the team by rebounding, playing tenacious defense, running the fast break, and so on. These activities demonstrate that the success of any individual is dependent upon teamwork. In the same way, a softball coach lets her backup pitcher know that she will be valuable to the team by using her in specific game situations.

Coaches who are good communicators also clearly state their expectations about behavior, effort, and fan conduct to their players and par-

Effective coaches are excellent communicators and are able to make their players feel positive about themselves and their team even in the face of adversity. (Bob Updegrove)

ents. By making sure that everyone is on the same page, good coaches help to eliminate numerous problems that could potentially creep up during the season. If a basketball coach asks that parents do not try to give their sons or daughters advice about playing time while they are sitting on the bench during games, he can save all the various parties involved from an embarrassing scene. But what is the best way to communicate with parents?

My own approach to communicating with parents has changed over the years. When I first got into coaching I would try to limit my dealings with parents to a bare minimum. As a young head coach, I didn't want to talk to people twice my age about how I ran my practices, my personal athletic experiences, or playing time. The problem with this approach is that parents end up guessing why you run your program the way you do, because you haven't told them about your philosophy and goals for the team. This can lead to dissension or loss of control or respect. And don't be fooled: parents can be very closely involved in their children's athletic lives, no matter what the level or age group. If you think a mother's concern about the playing time of her son on your T-ball team is unrealistic given the age of the athletes, it may be very real to the parent.

My approach to communicating with parents now is opposite to the method I employed my first few years coaching. I make myself available to talk to parents any time, with some exceptions. I explain to parents at our Meet the Coach Night, which takes place a week or two into practices, that they may contact me to discuss their son at any time except during practice or games, or immediately following games (when emotions of players, parents, and coaches are often running high). I hand out my business card, which has my home phone number, my cell phone number, and my e-mail address on it, so that parents can contact me at their convenience (as long as it does not conflict with the few situations I mentioned). I want to give parents every opportunity to discuss their son or daughter with me so they can have an understanding of the decisions I make when coaching our team.

A phone call from an unhappy parent is never an easy conversation. I do ask that parents discuss only the current season. I tell parents that I will not talk about their child with another parent so I ask that they extend to others the same courtesy. And conversations between a coach and parent do not always lead to an agreement by the end of the phone call, and they do not have to. A parent is entitled to share his or her feelings about why they feel their son or daughter should get more playing time, or whatever is their concern, and it is the job of the head coach to determine which players give his team the best chance for success. I see no reason why a coach should be afraid or unwilling to share his rationale for this with a parent, since an effective coach already speaks clearly and honestly to his athletes.

Another valuable tool for communicating with athletes is having an individual conversation or conference. Typically I try to meet one-on-one with my players once before the season and once after the season. Depending on how a season progresses, I have had years where I have met with my players individually in the middle of a season. Items discussed in preseason meetings may include: the coach's expectations for that player's playing time, the player's individual goals for the upcoming season, a coach's recent observations of the player from practices and scrimmages, or questions from the player about where he or she could improve. Even if you are not coaching a school team, it is a good idea if possible to set aside a time and place to speak with your athletes on an individual basis, even if that means that you have to ask each athlete in turn to show up twenty minutes before a practice or stay for a few minutes afterward. Most athletes in youth programs don't get this kind of attention, and it can do a lot for team unity and mutual respect. Postseason one-on-ones may include items such as how a player feels their individual season went, their plans for offseason camps and conditioning, a player's goals for next season, or a coach's impressions of the player's season.

I teach my athletes about what our team has done successfully and what our team could still improve upon, regardless of whether we won or lost our most recent contest. I stress to my athletes some positive aspect no matter how poorly we may have executed plays in a recent loss, while following a big win, I still review areas that we need to improve upon. I hope that athletes learn to evaluate their own performance in this same way. Basically, you're not as bad as your last poor performance, and you're probably not as good as your most recent success.

A final note about communication: it is just as important to allow your players the opportunity to share their ideas about their individual concerns. Rather than telling my players what I think about their season, I always open any midseason or postseason one-on-one conference by asking each player, "How do you feel about your individual season?" Sometimes I am surprised by the answers that I hear. I may learn that a player who I feel has had a good year is actually disappointed because he expected more of himself, or I may hear from a player that he is very satisfied with his efforts when I thought he might have done more.

It is essential to clearly state to your staff, players, and parents your ideas before and during a season as to how you feel the season should progress. Just as important as your ability to share your ideas with your staff, players, and parents is your willingness to listen to those same people in return.

Effective coaches are very well organized and have a strong work ethic.

This sounds obvious, but it is important always to try to maintain these qualities. With busy schedules, unforeseen events, or other unexpected demands on your daily routine, it can be more difficult than you might assume. Unless it comes naturally, effective coaches learn to stay organized. They can remember the numerous little things that need to be done to run a successful program. If a head coach is not organized, their assistant coaches, volunteer helpers, or players may have to do extra work to pick up the slack.

A high school baseball coach, as an example, needs on game day: his entire uniform (hat, jersey, pants, belt, socks, shoes), the scorebook, his stopwatch, pencils, his completed lineup card, the medical kit, scouting charts of his team's opponent, his glove for throwing batting practice, and his fungo bat to hit ground balls. Beyond being responsible for himself, the coach is responsible for making sure that every one of his fourteen to sixteen players has all their individual equipment, that they get on the bus in a timely fashion, and that that they bring all the necessary team equipment such as baseballs, helmets, catcher's gear, water, and ice.

Staying organized and on top of a commitment to a youth league team can be extremely difficult for a volunteer coach who does not teach at the school his players attend. This makes communicating ideas to players about practices, games, and team events even more difficult than it is for a school coach who gets the opportunity to see and talk to his players occasionally throughout the school day. There are several ways that a volunteer coach can stay organized so when he shows up at the ball field he is confident that his coaching staff, players, and their parents are all prepared.

The first way a coach can get organized is by doing as much work as possible before the season starts. By meeting with coaches, players, and parents ahead of time to discuss practice dates and times, game dates and times, individual and team equipment needs, and fees due to the league for participation, a volunteer coach can save countless hours of work and frustration once a season

Volunteer coaches know that they must commit themselves to long hours. Learning to stay organized and using time as efficiently as possible helps both the coach and their players. (Bob Updegrove)

begins. The second way a volunteer coach can stay organized is by setting up and using a phone tree or e-mail tree. If a volunteer coach is at his place of employment and a practice time or game time is moved or cancelled due to inclement weather he can simply call the first player or family on the phone tree to communicate the change of schedule. Each player will contact the next player on the list via phone or e-mail until everyone knows about the altered schedule. A third and final way a volunteer coach can stay organized is by enlisting his assistants and parents to help with dropping off and picking up players from practice and games, organizing team events like postgame snacks or drinks for players, facility maintenance duties involving mowing or raking the field after practice, fundraising, setting up team functions, and so on. The more a head coach can use these methods to help him stay organized, the more he can focus on the best ways to coach the players on his team.

Effective coaches also practice what they preach to their athletes in terms of being dedicated and working at their game year round. A coach has to make exactly the same decision that all players have to make. They can work to develop their talent during the season, or they can work at their skills all year. The days of showing up on the first day of the season and expecting to succeed are long gone.

During the season, countless tasks can test a coach's dedication. There are long bus rides following away games, watching and breaking down video of your own players or your opponents, creating scouting reports, washing uniforms, and reviewing game statistics, to name a few. Most coaches of quality high school programs require their players to practice six days per week. Beyond the two-hour routine practice, good programs involve weight lifting during the season after practices are over, as well as Saturday practices that help teams catch up or review skills that did not get covered throughout the week. Maintenance of baseball facilities during the season can involve mowing grass, raking dirt infields, tamping and watering batter's boxes and pitching mounds, and seeding and laying sod over well-used areas. Head coaches should expect the same dedication and work ethic from their assistant coaches as they do from themselves.

Developing a coaching work ethic, while maintaining family and work priorities, is a challenge that all coaches face. The best way to describe the effort is that it is a balancing act. Coaches must dedicate themselves to all three areas. As much as I would enjoy spending all day on a basketball court or athletic field working with youngsters, it would not be acceptable for me, my family, or the players. Most of us know of people who spend the overwhelming majority of their time and effort at the office; they often have little or no time for family commitment or for other activities like coaching. Coaches need to manage their time so they can fulfill their family and employment obligations prior to stepping into their role as a coach.

Once you have made the commitment to serve as a coach, you need to be there for your players. If it weren't for the countless sacrifices and dedication of my two high school coaches, I would not have developed to my full potential as an athlete or as a person. If a few infielders asked for extra ground balls after practice, one of our coaches would stay and hit us repetitions until we were exhausted. When one of us wanted to take extra batting practice, our coaches would pull out the batting tunnel to allow us to get as many swings as possible. During the time I played sports in high school, weight lifting programs were not commonly used in that level of athletics, but my teammates and I would ask our coaches to open up the weight room several days a week following practices so we could maintain and improve our strength. Our coaches always obliged our requests.

Why wouldn't a coach want his athletes to stay hours after practice to improve their skills? I did not fully appreciate the answer to this until I became a head coach. Coaches lead lives away from sports just like their athletes. Following a full day at work and a two-hour practice session, the prospect of spending another hour or two on the court or field isn't the first thing on many coaches' docket. Many coaches would rather head home to relax, and spend time with friends or family like anyone else who has finished work for the day.

It's hard to know where to draw the line. The coach who leaves the court or field the minute practice is over is often the same coach who argues that many of today's athletes aren't as dedicated as they used to be. If coaches are going to demand their athletes go above and beyond normal practice expectations, then they must be willing to have the same commitment. As important as this responsibility is to my players, I have divided putting in extra time with my players between myself and my assistant coaches.

If you are a parent volunteer as either a coach or assistant coach, stressing punctuality for practices is perhaps the best way to spend as much quality time with your athletes. In many youth or recreational leagues, volunteer coaches simply can't make the extra time commitment. That is OK, of course. Demonstrating the dedication to make it to practice on time, to use the time you have efficiently, and allowing your own behavior to help set an example with your athletes is just as important.

A volunteer or youth league coach is often crucial in the development of an athlete's talents because many athletes begin to develop their habits, whether they are good or bad, before they enter the realm of competitive school sports programs. If a volunteer coach can offer a little extra help after games or practice, that extra commitment to a young player not only develops skills but helps instill in the athlete a solid work ethic that will benefit that player in all aspects of his or her life, whether on the athletic field, the classroom, or a future career.

But no matter how busy or hectic life can get, an effective coach plans specific time each day to spend with his family, at work, and coaching his players. If he is unable to budget his time, then he may shortchange others, and ultimately, he is cheating himself.

To manage his time and the many demands of his team and other commitments, a coach needs to be well organized and have a strong work ethic.

Effective coaches run purposeful, efficient practices.

For every game or match that is played, no matter what the level or sport, there are many, many, more practice sessions. And it is practice that makes any accomplishment in a game a reality. Effective coaches get the most out of practice time. They make it clear to their staff and players that practice is not the time to go through the motions. They make sure that their coaches and players have an understanding that every aspect of practice has a distinct purpose that will help players and the team as a whole improve their performance.

Coaches who get the most out of their practice time normally have a typed practice plan in their hands. (A selection of sample practice plans can be found in the appendix.) Besides serving as a reference, a practice plan tells the staff and players that you spent time prior to practice planning what you want to accomplish with every minute during that day's session.

As a coach, the days I have walked onto the field or the court without a practice plan in my hands have been very few. I must confess that my plans have not always been as neatly composed as I might have wished. In fact, I wrote my plans by hand before I had access to a computer. Regardless, a major strength for any head coach is to have a definite, organized idea about how to run a good practice.

Having a plan in your hands helps you to do several things. First, a timed practice plan keeps you from spending too much time teaching one particular skill. Why is that a problem? Let's say that you have a two-hour practice slot because of Little League teams sharing the same facility or you have a high school field without lights. The only way to make sure you will cover all the various areas you need to without running out of time is to stay on schedule. Second, a practice plan serves as a written reminder to a coach regarding the areas he needs to cover with his team.

The sample practice plans may give you ideas on how to combine individual skills with team concepts. But don't worry if you can't come up with the perfect practice plan. Any good coach knows that they can't cover every situation that their team may face come game time. But an organized coach maintains a file of practice plans (either in a folder or on disk) so they know what has been covered in each day's practice. A coach can then assess what skills they need to review or teach during the future practice sessions. By simply adding a written note to your practice plan, following the completion of each day's practice, a coach can keep track of personal observations he makes during a specific practice. This can be helpful in planning the next day's practice session or future practices.

An efficient practice plan makes sure that as many of your players are active as possible during each practice session. For example, if you have 50 players on your junior high football team, but only the starting 11 players are on the field and you expect the other 39 to pay attention, watch intently, and ask insightful questions, then you have another thing coming. If, however, you have four squads of 11 players on each side of the ball rotating through different plays, then nearly all of your players are learning, improving, and getting in shape. Another example of a poor use of practice time involves nearly every Little League batting practice that I have ever witnessed. Normally, one player hits batting practice while the other 13 or so players supposedly play defense, while they pick daisies, kick dirt around the infield, or stare at the clouds. Instead, if the practice consists of two groups of seven players in each group, then six players rotate on the field playing defense while one hits; the other group of seven players are in groups of two or three hitting tennis balls off tees outside the fence. In this scenario, the six defensive players don't have time to daydream because they are too busy chasing down balls that are being hit all over the field. Meanwhile, the seven players who are not on the field get the opportunity to get numerous repetitions and practice their swing mechanics through tee drills.

Another point that a head coach should consider when planning practice is to make the best possible use of assistant or volunteer coaches. A head coach who is realistic and has his team and players' interests in mind knows that he cannot cover all the areas necessary to prepare for success on game day. Therefore, when developing practice plans, he makes sure to incorporate anyone who is willing and able to help his team: a dad who wants to throw batting practice or hit ground balls, an assistant coach who videotapes the scrimmage portion of hockey practice, or a volunteer who charts the number of tackles each player makes at football practice. Anyone who can consistently participate in the development of your team's athletes should be considered a valuable resource and included in the practice plan. If you are a volunteer coach, it is a good idea to see if any parents would want to assist you. School programs and some organized leagues have the luxury of assistant coaches as a matter of course. For recreational leagues, the coach can sometimes be the only person running a team's entire program, but it doesn't have to be that way. Make it a part of your overall plan to secure the help of other volunteers.

A final thought is that longer sessions don't necessarily result in better practices. Many young coaches believe that the longer their teams are on the field or court the better they will become. In many instances, the result can be just the opposite. If a coach has his team on the practice field for hours, his players can get bored, lose focus, and become less productive. Most effective coaches would rather have their team take part in a quality, quick-moving ninety-minute practice instead of standing around for the better part of a day making sure every player gets the necessary preparation for games. The age and attention span of the players should also enter into planning the length of practice sessions. A short, efficient, well-planned practice is better than any long, overextended one.

Coaches should run organized, timed practices that keep players active and working on a variety of skills.

Effective coaches have the courage to make difficult decisions, and to admit when they make mistakes.

While most coaches enjoy working with their staff and players, they must have the backbone to make some very difficult decisions. Imagine that you are a football coach facing the following scenario: Your best wide receiver shows up late for a key late-season game, missing the pregame talk. You know that you need to play him in order to have a chance at winning and you don't want to disappoint the rest of the players who have worked so hard to get to this point. Your dilemma: do you have him sit out the game because you, your assistants, and your players know that he has broken the team rules? Or do you go ahead and make an exception this time and play him?

Either way you choose to handle the situation, someone won't be happy. If you make your best wide receiver sit, you decrease your team's chances for success. You may also damage your relationship with your star player for the remainder of the season. If you let him play, you send him and the team a signal that achieving victory is more important than team rules. Beyond the mixed message you would be giving to your star player, the respect and credibility you have earned with your coaching staff and with the other players would be damaged.

A coach should not be trying to win a popularity contest. I could not imagine my college basketball coach starting off an early Saturday morning practice by asking for a show of hands of who would rather have the day off since they were out late the previous night. A coach has to make choices that are unpopular at times with his players because his decisions are for the good of the team.

Effective coaches know that instilling discipline in their athletes and their team means getting them to do things they would rather not do. Football coaches make players realize the importance of improving strength and speed, so athletes spend countless hours in the weight room pushing their bodies to the limit. Basketball coaches have their players do tiring defensive slides day after day. Baseball coaches have their players hit until their hands are calloused.

By getting players to push themselves past their comfort zone without physically jeopardizing their health, a good coach knows that they greatly increase their team's chances for success. Therefore, the football player who grudgingly went to the weight room in the off-season is able to drive his opponent off the line of scrimmage the next season. The basketball player who dreaded defensive slides waits eagerly for the opportunity to shut down her opponent with the game on the line without thinking about whether her legs can take it. The baseball hitter drives the ball through the gap when he gets a pitch he has practiced hitting thousands of times over the winter. By helping to instill the necessary discipline to help a player improve their work ethic, a coach helps a player improve his overall ability. This approach serves the individual athlete and his entire team better than if the coach took the easy way out and let his players off the hook.

But players and coaches are human, and sometimes teams don't play well, or a coach makes a mistake. Young or egotistical coaches may look to place blame everywhere but on themselves when things go wrong for their team. Saying "It was the referee's fault" or "These players have no heart" are ways that ineffective coaches divert attention from the fact that, in most cases, they could be doing a better job preparing their players in practice or leading them during games.

Effective coaches are able to analyze their own role in a team's struggles and make the necessary adjustments to get their team back on the path to success. If a coach's answer for getting their team out of a losing streak is to lengthen practice and increase the intensity of drills and scrimmages, as I naively did as a young coach, they are probably contributing to their team's misfortunes more than they realize. It is possible to push a team too hard. The answer may be to get the players' minds off their record with an occasional day off from practice (though that thought never crossed my mind in the first few years that I coached).

Effective coaches will not make excuses, nor will they allow their players to make excuses when things don't go their way. The easiest people in the world to blame for an individual or team's misfortunes are umpires or referees. There is one problem with this logic: umpires and referees do not play on the opposing team. They are volunteers or underpaid folks who give their time to ensure fair play. I would be a wealthy man if I had a dime for each time I have heard a basketball coach say, "The ref cost us the game." My response would be: Did he shoot two out of ten from the free-throw line in the last quarter, or was that a player? I have heard football coaches blame a loss on a call by a referee; but did his team's three fumbles and two interceptions have more to do with the game's outcome than an officiating call? I am intentionally being sarcastic, but coaches should be most concerned with the decisions that they make or the plays that their own team executes or fails to execute.

An inexperienced coach may believe that he should never admit making a mistake to his players because they might not respect his future decisions with the team. I have found from personal experience that most players find it refreshing when a coach acknowledges that they could be doing a better job. For example, I have told my baseball team that I hurt our chances for victory by telling a player to steal a base; he was then thrown out to end a potential rally for our team. By owning up to my overzealousness on the base paths, I remove the focus of our team's loss from my players' bruised egos and allow them to put the loss on my shoulders as well.

> A good coach has the courage to make his athletes do what is necessary to improve, even if the decision is not popular. Effective coaches understand that if they expect their players to learn from their mistakes and be held accountable, they should hold themselves and their staff members to the same high standards.

Effective coaches assess their team's strengths and weaknesses and then play to their strengths.

This is easier said than done in certain sports. In the majority of sports where the team on offense

Effective coaches make necessary adjustments to get their team or a player back on track toward the goals they have set. (BRHS)

possesses the ball, a coach will do everything they can to get the ball into their most talented player's hands to give their team the best chance for success.

Depending on the sport and the makeup of their team a coach has to make some important decisions about how to give their team its best chances for success. A basketball coach may have ten offensive plays. Eight of these plays may have the ball end up in his best shooter's hands for a wide open fifteen-foot jump shot. A football coach who believes his team can run the ball consistently may line up his best athletes as running backs instead of at quarterback or wide receiver, where they would not be involved in as many yardage-gaining plays as he would like.

Depending on the strengths and weaknesses of each year's team, an effective coach may alter their approach. If a baseball coach has a team that is loaded with fast players, he might spend the last ten minutes of each practice working on base stealing. If his players lack the necessary speed to steal bases consistently, then he may have his team practice the hit-and-run every day in batting practice so they can execute it successfully in games. Maybe his team lacks big players who swing for the fences, so he has his players bunt their way to victory.

Another important reason you need to know your team's strengths and weaknesses is so you can help your team improve in areas where they struggle. An effective softball coach, for example, may alter defensive-oriented practices that have been successful in past seasons in order to help her team practice the skills necessary to score runs consistently. A basketball coach who lacks consistent perimeter shooters may incorporate shooting drills in each day's warm-ups at practice in an effort to improve her team's area of weakness. Her team may still play to its strength of getting the ball inside to its post players come game time, but at least the team will steadily improve in another way so their attack is not so one-dimensional.

> A coach determines what style of play gives his team the best chance for success, and then does everything possible to have his players follow this particular strategy.

Effective coaches understand that their playing careers are over.

Coaches should understand that in order to dedicate their effort, time, and energy to their players, they must accept that their own playing days are over. In fact, if a coach's competitive desire is so great that they must prove their worth on a playing field, there are plenty of other ways to do this. Many coaches who are former athletes take up activities such as running, weight lifting, golf, and tennis, in order to fulfill their competitive desires after their primary athletic careers are over. If coaches do not accept some sort of closure to their own playing days, the risk of reliving the glory days through their players increases.

A youth league coach may feel that the best way to teach young players a particular skill is by modeling the fundamental in front of his athletes. This makes sense; by showing players how to perform a skill, a coach visually demonstrates to his players the way to execute a certain task. Problems arise, however, if the coach tries to outdo his players or show off by turning teaching skills into competitive situations with his players. By seeing how many shots they can make or how many home runs they can hit, coaches are not demonstrating to their players how to execute skills, but they are trying to reassure themselves that they still have the talent that made them great athletes years ago.

Coaches who use themselves as teaching examples for their players take the focus away from the players. As someone who teaches and coaches young people, I have learned that the last thing a young athlete wants to hear is ancient history about the coach's playing days.

Effective coaches who want to get the best out of their team make sure the focus is on their players' talents, not on their own past athletic efforts.

Effective coaches are always looking to learn and improve their skills.

Effective coaches know that the day they think they know it all is the day they start getting out coached. Don't get me wrong—there is no need to reinvent the wheel: 95 percent of skills are taught the same way from year to year. But coaches who look for ways to get better as coaches will inevitably find new ways to help their teams succeed. In Chapter 4, "Learning from Other Coaches," ideas are offered regarding the importance of coaches being willing to learn and improve by listening to others. Nearly every coaching video I have watched and every coach I have heard at various clinics uses some variation of this statement: "If you learn one new thing today that makes you a better coach, then it was worth your time, money, and effort." As many times as I have heard this, I still believe it is true.

If, as a head basketball coach, you decide that you are satisfied with your team's performance in every area except scoring on the fast break, then you should go listen to the best speakers at the high school, college, and professional levels explain their methods of fast-break offense at every clinic you can get to. I played on a high school basketball team that averaged nearly 80 points per game mainly by executing a fast-break drill that my high school coach had us practice every day of my senior year. If you are not effectively coaching your own players in a particular area, then you should do everything you can do to learn other methods to teach that skill.

The opportunity to learn from another coach may not be a formal clinic; you can seek out people with expertise on your own. Having never trained in a formal, regimented weight lifting program as an athlete, I decided that I needed to research and learn about the best ways to increase my players' athletic abilities through weight training. I spent three days trailing Dan Riley, who at the time was the strength and conditioning coach for the Washington Redskins. I tried to learn as much as I possibly could about nutrition, muscle building, and differences in various weight lifting programs as I asked Riley every question that came to my mind and took notes. Riley was generous with his time and did as much as he could to educate me about the positives, negatives, and myths of the various weight lifting programs. It is important to remember that there are many knowledgeable people in other programs who can be a very beneficial resource for coaches who want to improve their skills.

Another way coaches can improve the number of strategies at their disposal is by watching teams play games on television or in person. Studying plays in televised games allows a coach to add new strategies to their base of knowledge. Numerous "geniuses" can be studied by watching their game plans unfold on television: Phil Jackson has made a living getting teams to execute his version of the triangle offense, Urban Meyer gained national notoriety with his success at Utah using the spread offense, Jim Boeheim has taken Syracuse to national prominence by mastering the 2-3 half court zone defense, to name just a few. There are numerous plays and strategies that a coach can see develop from a spectator's viewpoint that may influence the way they make decisions the next time a game situation arises. Although watching college or professional players can be a way to learn new strategies, expecting high school or youth league players to be able to simulate these same actions with the same ease is unrealistic. Two strategies that I have seen work on televised games that I have employed while coaching include the suicide squeeze bunt in baseball and last-second plays designed to help a team take a good shot at the end of basketball games.

A youth league coach who is going to work with a group of second and third graders should try to see in advance a game at the level or in the league in which he will be coaching. Likewise it is a good idea for a new high school basketball coach who may have played competitive basketball ten or fifteen years ago to attend a few games in the league or conference to see the level of play that his players will bring to the table. In addition to seeing the quality and types of athletes and any changes in style that have occurred in the game, a new coach can see what strategies work for the players he will soon be teaching.

Effective coaches realize that they need to take the time, effort, and energy to learn through clinics and workshops or other teams' games.

Effective coaches make playing sports fun for their athletes and enjoy coaching.

The idea of "working" at a game as an eight-, ten-, or twelve-year old may help explain why an overwhelming number of young athletes quit sports by the time they enter their teenage years. Coaches should make playing games fun for their athletes.

Athletes today have many more options for spending their free time than did most current coaches who were growing up in the 1970s or 1980s. If an athlete today is unhappy with his coach, teammates, or playing time, he may play for one of the numerous barnstorming teams available in many areas, may spend his free time playing video games or surfing the Internet, or may quit playing sports altogether. These various options were not as readily available when many current coaches grew up. The bottom line is this: if a young person is not enjoying playing on your team, the chances of that athlete continuing their athletic career or even giving a genuine effort during the present season are severely decreased.

Coaches today need to be much more creative in planning practices to make sure that today's athletes are more involved and active than in years past. Most athletes want to feel that they are truly part of a team concept. If players spend most of basketball practice rebounding for the team's best shooter or shagging batting practice balls for the baseball team's best hitter, then they will most likely find other ways to spend their time. Practices that involve equal participation from all the players on a team typically are much more enjoyable for everyone.

Coaches who try to keep their players happy during practice are willing to experiment with new, different methods to alter the normal routine players are used to. I have seen basketball coaches who allow players to loosen up the first few minutes of practice while listening to music played through the public address system. Using the scoreboard to keep track of touchdowns scored

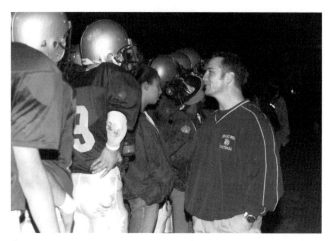

Coaching is one of the most rewarding experiences for those who enjoy sports. (BRHS)

during a goal line drill is a great way to pick up the intensity level at a junior high football practice. Finishing baseball practice by letting players hit opposite-handed is a way to lighten the mood the day after a tough loss.

The importance of making practices enjoyable cannot be underestimated. Many athletes will be surprised by what they end up learning during "fun" practices. For example, my first Little League baseball coach was able to explain to us and show us the fundamentals of how to play baseball correctly, but he made learning the game fun by developing skills through contests. For example, instead of making players field ground balls repeatedly in what may seem like a boring drill, he would see who could make the most plays in a row. Sometimes, he would divide us into two teams to see which group of players could make the most plays successfully. By turning drill sessions into contests, our Little League coach was getting us to work at becoming better players; we just didn't realize it because we were focused on competing and having fun. Now that I am a high school coach, I am amazed at the number of kids who enter ninth grade who have no idea how to perform fundamental aspects of baseball—throwing a baseball in a straight line, catching ground balls and fly balls with two hands, bunting, running the bases, knowing what base to throw to—skills that I learned while having fun at practice. Making it enjoyable to practice and learn a sport is not as common as it should be.

At the college level, or even with serious high school varsity competitors, it's easy to understand the concept of "working at your game." The problem with telling or forcing a nine-year-old to work at a sport or a particular skill is that it isn't any fun for a young person, but "playing" is. The trick to being an effective coach with young kids, as my Little League coach obviously knew, is getting your players to work hard to improve without realizing it.

As a high school coach, I now use a number of strategies in an effort to keep our players motivated and focused during practices while still having fun. We end many practices with some sort of competition. By having our players practice a skill like bunting through a contest, I accomplish several things: my team members practice the particular skill they need to improve; my players perform in a pressure situation; and the contests promote team chemistry.

As much as I want players entering high school to be fundamentally sound as baseball players, it is equally important that they have the passion and desire to learn and play the game. A Little League coach who makes practices and games fun for his athletes encourages his players to compete in their sport for years to come. In contrast, if players at the youth league level are constantly embarrassed or criticized by overzealous coaches or through tedious, complex, or overwhelming practices, the chance of these young people continuing to play their sport is severely diminished. They are also losing out on a fun childhood experience.

The flip side is that coaches themselves must enjoy coaching. They should have fun teaching players during practice and should not be afraid to enjoy getting caught up in the moment of a great game. I am a firm believer that the day a coach (whether a volunteer or a paid professional) starts to view coaching as work, instead of as a passion, they should get out of coaching.

Effective coaches work with young people year in and year out, not because they have to, but because they want to. As a coach, I look forward to the numerous teaching opportunities that athletics provide me. I know that there are lessons about dedication, hard work, and sacrifice that I can teach my athletes and teams that I would be hard pressed to simulate in the classroom. This is part of the fun of teaching and coaching young people.

Having fun while being involved in athletics at any level is contagious. By having fun while coaching you are setting the best example for young athletes, who should enjoy playing sports at any age.

All of these principles apply to coaching at every level, and it is my hope that one or more of them will end up helping you improve your own team's chances for success and your personal quest to becoming an even better coach. There are some principles of coaching that are specific to higher-level sports programs and athletes of high-school age and older, and those will be taken up in the next chapter.

3

Principles of Effective Coaching for Advanced Players or Elite Programs

Playing sports is like a pyramid. At the lower levels like Little League, everyone has to play. In junior high school, the better players play. But as you move up the pyramid (to competitive high school and college athletics) only the best of the best earn the right to play.—Jack Bruen

The following principles are geared more toward coaching advanced players, older players, and in programs like AAU that tend to be more sophisticated than youth leagues. The majority of these principles will directly affect the amount of success, in terms of wins and losses, that your team will experience. Therefore, this chapter sets out to explain some of the key areas that many coaches use, especially when coaching "higher level" amateur teams.

Principles of Effective Coaching

Effective coaches of advanced players or elite teams. . .

1. Get players to follow their "system."

2. Are not afraid to push or discipline their most talented player.

3. Understand that their team is only as strong as its weakest link.

4. Work year-round with players in their program.

5. Constantly improve and upgrade their program yearly.

Effective coaches get players to follow their "system."

In the NCAA Division I men's basketball championship game in 2003, Syracuse won playing a 2-3 half court zone defense. Syracuse's coach, Jim Boeheim, the longest tenured Division I men's basketball coach in the country, has one philosophy regarding what it takes to win: an aggressive 2-3 half court zone defense. He has been following this strategy for nearly three decades. This is his system and if you want to play for him, you have to be willing to play it. A great college coach like Boeheim recruits certain athletes that fit his particular program. He then teaches and drills these athletes in the various aspects of his style of play, and his players then do their best to execute his directives. The more that your players believe in the way your system works, the better your chances are for success with your entire team. What is the advantage of having a coaching "system"? Effective coaches teach their players systematically so that if a starting player is removed from the lineup for any reason, then a backup player can be inserted into the lineup and the team will continue to play effectively. Many junior varsity and varsity baseball teams use the same offensive and defensive signals from the dugout, from the catcher to the pitcher, and so on. This means that when a junior varsity player comes up to the varsity team, all the coach has to do is issue the player a varsity uniform. Every signal, every word of terminology, every pick off play, is exactly the same between the two teams. By teaching all players the same system, a coaching staff makes the transition for players to the varsity team go as smoothly as possible.

Another way that coaches develop their systems is by having players of different ages and skill levels in their program practice together. By having a ninth-grade second baseman on the junior varsity practice double plays with an eleventh-grade shortstop who starts on the varsity team, a coach enhances the younger player's skill development, which ultimately leads to his program's continued success in future seasons.

Effective coaches are not afraid to push or discipline their players, even the most talented player(s).

All players, regardless of their talent level, should be treated equally. Numerous coaches find it extremely difficult to keep this in mind since winning is so attractive and coaching a highly talented athlete is rewarding in its own right.

There are several reasons why coaches need to push their most talented players as hard as anyone else on their team. First, it sends a message to all the players on the team that regardless of their varying degrees of talent, all members of a team are expected to put forth their best effort. If the best player on the basketball team doesn't run the last sprint of conditioning, yet still is the starter in tomorrow's game, what does that tell their teammates? This type of "mixed message" is bad for everyone on the team ranging from your star player to the least talented person on the roster.

Another reason a coach should not bend the rules for their best player is that it tells the player that a talented athlete does not have to work as hard as the less skilled players. An athlete determines that since he can score twenty points per night or throw a fastball eighty-five miles per hour, his natural talent will compensate for his lack of hustle, focus, or dedication. Such a lack of good work ethic is destined for serious disappointment and failure. We have all heard stories of ath-

A coach needs to treat all players equally, even the most talented ones, and in order to maintain both effectiveness and respect, a coach cannot be afraid to discipline anyone on the team. (BRHS)

letes who have been coddled and told how special they are: starting at home, it continues through youth league, oftentimes through AAU, high school, and college. The problem is that sooner or later a naturally talented athlete faces an opponent who is just as fast, strong, or skilled as he or she is. Then what does that player have to rely on? Can he outwork his opponent? Probably not, due to the fact that he never developed a reliable work ethic during years of lackluster practice sessions. Can she outwit her opponent? Probably not, because she has constantly relied on being more talented than her normal opposition so she has never developed the mental toughness needed to succeed when facing real adversity. A coach who turns a blind eye to weaknesses in a talented player's character is not only doing a disservice to the team; in the long run, the coach is reinforcing the traits that bring many former athletes crashing down, particularly when they believe the same treatment extended to them in the sports world will carry over to a future job situation.

Beyond helping players to develop their talents, an effective coach must occasionally be willing to perform a task that may very well harm their team's short-term chances for victory: disciplining an athlete. In the case of negative behavior involving the best athlete, a coach must ask himself if he is willing to discipline his best player when he knows he will severely lessen the team's chances for success.

I have heard both sides of this issue from players, coaches, and parents. One line of thinking is that disciplining your best athlete for breaking a team rule such as missing practice can be handled by some additional conditioning. By doing this, a message has been sent to the athlete that his or her decision to miss practice is unacceptable to you as a coach. This leaves the door open for a coach to allow the star athlete to play in future games since he or she has been forced to accept responsibility and consequences for making a poor decision. On the contrary, the strict, old-school train of thought is that if a player doesn't practice, he or she doesn't play. This is a highly effective coaching tool that sends the message to all players on a team that if you want the opportunity to play on game night, you must be willing to fulfill your commitment to the team by participating in all required practice sessions. As a coach you have to ask yourself what decision you are willing to make regarding disciplining an athlete, especially when the player who has exercised poor judgment is your best player. I have heard coaches say, "You can't punish the whole team by benching your best player, because if you do it affects everyone's chances to be successful on game night." Other coaches argue, "The only players who should be allowed the privilege of competing in games are the players who can show up for practice on time, support their teammates, and listen to their coaches."

For me, playing time is earned, which means it can be taken away. If a player on my team can't show up for school, class, or practice on time, listen to his teachers or coaches, and make a genuine effort in the classroom and on the athletic field, he should not be allowed to represent his teammates, his coach, his family, or his school in athletic competition. Beyond that, why would a basketball coach want a player who doesn't treat his teachers with respect to play on his team? This player would also most likely be disrespectful of referees, teammates, and coaches. Would a baseball coach want a player who is always late to school or practice to be his leadoff hitter? I doubt it. If a young person can't get to school or class on time, would

I count on him making it to the bus on time for an away game? Not a chance. I agree with what my high school baseball coach, Wayne Todd, told me years ago, "Kids need structure. They want structure. Kids want to be told when they do something right and they need to be told when they do something wrong."

Discipline is an area on which effective coaches refuse to compromise. If the idea of sports as a teaching tool is to prepare young people for life, then we have failed a student-athlete when we turn a blind eye to their poor judgment. I do not care if a young man is our team's best athlete, or our team's only realistic chance for success on game night. If an athlete acts in a manner that represents himself, his teammates, his coaches, his family, or his school negatively, then that athlete will have to deal with the consequences for his actions. Whether it is a loss of playing time or extra conditioning for minor problems or a game suspension or dismissal from the team for major infractions, it remains a coach's job to teach his players how to play, how to hustle, and how to behave.

If a youth league coach leaves a player who will not accept coaching or work within the team concept on the court or field, then the coach is ultimately doing the athlete a disservice. If an athlete is allowed at a young age to act inappropriately and the coach won't take them out of the game or sit them on the bench, the athlete will probably believe that in future situations they will not have to follow the rules. The lesson learned by the athlete is that they can do whatever they want. While a youth league coach may choose to pass the buck and overlook bad behavior, the overwhelming majority of high school coaches will not allow these types of behaviors to slide which may come as a shock to an athlete who has not been disciplined.

School coaches would be well-served to state clearly their expectations for their student-athletes' behavior prior to the start of the season at their "Preseason Night" or "Meet the Coach Night." By clearly stating the expectations for behavior ahead of time, a coach who disciplines an athlete is more likely to receive parental support than if they wait to announce their view on discipline until after an incident has occurred. Even if a school coach wanted to turn a blind eye to poor behavior by an athlete, athletic directors and administrators usually do not. Therefore, if an athlete learns the lessons of discipline at a young age, they will avoid countless occurrences of trouble in future events. As a junior high school or high school athlete, a young person who has been "spoiled" by soft treatment by their Little League coaches will most likely be in for quite a surprise when a school coach applies discipline for items like being late to practice or displaying a poor attitude. Also, the more a coach of young athletes reinforces consistent discipline, the more they help to dispel the notion that there will be any future "star treatment" for certain athletes.

A first-time coach may think that disciplining an athlete is easier said than done. I don't know if that's true. I never enjoy benching a player for a game, or making them perform extra conditioning, but it certainly is not difficult to do. I simply ask myself, "What am I teaching this player and the members of my team by making my decision?" Whenever I consider this question, the fact that my team may not win their next game because my star player's behavior has forced me to place him on the bench doesn't seem to matter quite as much to me.

Simply put, coaching athletics at the youth, junior high, and high school level should be a tool for teaching kids. Coaches are supposed to teach players sportsmanship. We are supposed to show athletes the right way to handle winning and losing. We are supposed to show them how to become better athletes. This all contributes to teaching young athletes how to become better people.

An effective coach puts his ego and his desire to win aside, and makes the decision to discipline their athletes, regardless of their talent, when it is necessary. Disciplining an athlete is what is best for your team and for the individual you coach (whether they like it or not).

Effective coaches understand that their team is only as strong as its weakest link.

No matter how talented their team's best athletes may be, a coach must spend as much time, if not more time, developing their lesser talented players. There are several reasons why good coaches need to dedicate their time, effort, and energy equally to all the players on the team. First, on a team everyone should be treated the same. If a different set of rules or expectations is applied to the best player or the athlete on the end of the bench, players will receive conflicting messages as to what is expected of them. Second, the roles of players are constantly changing. For example, if your best player on a basketball team is in foul trouble, losing or winning a game in the fourth quarter may very well depend on how the back up players perform in a very high pressure situation. That being the case, it is essential for your team's success to make sure your back-up players receive the same amount of repetitions, the same amount of praise and criticism, and the same amount of attention that you pay to your starters. It is only fair to push these athletes just as hard as your starters if you want them to give you the same effort. Third, injuries happen. If your starting quarterback twists his ankle in the middle of a game halfway through the season and your back-up quarterback hasn't taken a practice snap since summer camp, you and your team are in trouble.

In contrast, if you have made sure that your back-up quarterback has practiced with the second team offense all season, and occasionally you have given him some repetitions with the first team, your situation is slightly more manageable.

Another reason to dedicate an equal amount of time and energy to all your players is that different athletes progress at different rates. I have coached numerous baseball players who entered our school as physically small, limited athletes who left as solid, varsity starters four years later. These changes are due to a number of factors, but the most obvious is that young people grow by leaps and bounds through their teenage years. If a player who comes into our program as a 5'3, 110-pound player has a growth spurt while spending the course of several years in our weight program, he may be a 6'0, 175-pound athlete by the time he enters his junior or senior year.

A player who starts playing on a Little League baseball team at age nine will be a totally different player and person when he is the leader of that team as a twelve-year-old. If that athlete feels that his coaches don't try to help him because he is too small or weak at age nine, then he will never reach his full potential by the time he is age twelve. I have also witnessed the opposite trend, where athletes who are too heavy as they enter high school change their diet and workout routine to become much improved athletes over time. Again, an effective head coach has to be willing to

Coaches should dedicate an equal amount of time to all their players since athletes progress at different rates. (Bob Updegrove)

allow an athlete to improve physically if they want to see that athlete reach their full potential.

The key to having athletes change for the better in your program is this—they have to feel that it is worth their time to improve athletically. If a second baseman is told at the end of his freshman year, "You're not a bad player, but you're never going to be a good varsity player because you're too short," it is safe to say that athlete won't make much of an effort to improve his athleticism. If the same athlete is told by his coach, "I think you have excellent baseball skills, but you are going to have to dedicate yourself to improving yourself in all areas of the sport, including your physical conditioning," that athlete is more likely to be motivated for the tremendous effort needed to achieve his goals.

An effective coach understands that working with the least talented or most physically challenged athletes on their team or in their program oftentimes has a major effect on their team's performance. There is no crystal ball which tells us how athletes will develop, so coaches should do all they can to aid each one of their player's progress. Remember: if you as a coach do not take the time or make the effort to help your less talented players, your opponents will surely take advantage of these same players' weaknesses on game night.

Effective coaches work year-round with the players in their program.

In today's athletic world, if a coach and their players are not constantly doing something to improve their skills and program, they will be falling behind the competition. This is definitely a balancing act. It is evident that numerous young athletes are quitting certain sports because they are playing year-round at a young age and experiencing "burnout." A coach should impress upon their players that they should continue to improve as an athlete year-round, but they do not have to concentrate on their main sport. If a player has a desire to participate in another sport in the off-season, a coach should support that athlete. The same concepts of discipline, teamwork, and sportsmanship are taught by nearly all team coaches. But if an athlete does not play a sport during the off-season, a coach should suggest that the athlete get involved in a weight training and/or running program which will improve his strength and flexibility and reduce his chances of injury. (Proper weight lifting and safe training techniques will be discussed in Chapter 8.)

Starting in September, the prospective players in our program lift weights three days a week after school—every Monday, Wednesday, and Friday. Beginning in January and leading up to tryouts at the end of February, many of the prospective players in our program attend an indoor winter hitting camp. This allows athletes who are participating in high school basketball or wrestling to hone their baseball skills without interfering with the commitment they made to their winter team. During our season, from March through May, we are involved in a combination of practicing, playing games, and lifting weights six days a week. During the summer our players play a mix of Little League, Babe Ruth, and AAU, depending on their age and ability. The only exceptions to this year-round program are those athletes who play a fall or winter sport. In those cases, the break from playing only one sport helps players to avoid burnout from focusing on one sport twelve months of the year.

Other sports, such as basketball, also have similar year-round activities, with opportunities for players to attend summer camps and partici- pate in various fall, spring, and summer leagues.

In addition to participating in these camps, coaches can see the players on travel league and house league teams that will one day attend their high schools. Also, many times these programs run fundraisers to upgrade items like uniforms and to pay for team meals for their players. These off-season leagues are essential to the development of the talent and chemistry of sub-varsity players. They are also an opportunity for coaches to demonstrate fundamental basketball drills, offensive sets, defensive strategies, practice expectations, etc., in an effort to prepare the players for entering high school.

In addition to year-round commitments for players, effective coaches understand that a key to being a good leader during the season is directly related to the amount of time they spend preparing themselves before the season starts. The numerous tasks that come up during the season severely limit the chances to make major coaching adjustments in the middle of a season. Therefore, the more time that a coach spends in the preseason preparing himself, his staff, and his players for the upcoming season, the more efficiently he will able to coach his team during the season.

In the course of a typical preseason a coach must address the following:

- equipment needs
- meetings with assistants

- preparing and typing playbooks
- scheduling practices and games
- creating team rules

Anyone who has coached knows that there are no short cuts for these major preseason tasks. These items need to be discussed and revisited repeatedly before a head coach can make a final decision. For example, if a softball coaching staff wants to order new equipment for the upcoming season, they must start by taking an inventory of their current equipment and its condition. After assessing the condition of the previous year's tees, balls, helmets, bases, catching gear, uniforms, etc., they must then take the time to research what companies carry the new, desired equipment for the upcoming season. The staff must then price out the various pieces of equipment and find the best possible value to make sure they don't waste dollars from their league or school budget. After ordering and receiving the equipment, the staff must catalog and store the new items until the season starts.

Another valuable use of the preseason takes place when coaches gather to share ideas and information. This allows every member of the staff to be on the same page in areas ranging from how to perform a fundamental skill of a particular sport to items like team rules. An effective coach meets with his assistants to discuss as many situations as possible so the entire staff has a uniform vision as to how they will teach various skills. A preseason meeting of a basketball staff, for example, may include topics like: man-to-man offensive plays, zone offensive plays, in-bounds scoring plays, sidelines in-bounds plays, press break in-bounds plays, man-to-man defense, zone defense, full court press defense, etc. Every member of the staff should be familiar with the skills, terminology, and responsibilities of each coach and player in each of these numerous situations. Discussing and explaining these numerous areas may seem like a daunting task, but it is time well spent to avoid confusion and frustration for players and coaches alike when the first practices begin.

Following a season, a coach should meet with their staff members individually as well as in a group setting to get their feedback on the recently concluded season, and to get their thoughts on the upcoming season. If a head coach gives assistants a genuine opportunity to share their ideas regarding the program's philosophy, personnel, and future, they have not only learned more about their program, but they have ensured that their assistant coaches feel that their thoughts and concerns are heard. Notes from these postseason meetings serve as a starting point for the next season's preseason sessions.

Effective coaches constantly improve and upgrade their program yearly.

Improving the overall athletic program is an aspect of coaching that does not necessarily show up in the wins and losses column; rather, it is a point of pride and professionalism that assistant coaches, players, and parents will recognize and appreciate. In addition it is a good way to raise team morale.

Think of the numerous ways that a head basketball coach of a junior high team could enhance a regular basketball season that normally consists of just practices and games. Some examples are: printing a game program, getting local restaurants to sponsor team meals, purchasing new practice uniforms, having an intrasquad scrimmage to kick off the season, repainting the gymnasium, hanging the name of every player on the varsity team beneath the scoreboard, and hosting a players versus alumni game. Obviously, it would be very difficult to do all these extra features in one season, but the head coach could choose a few of these extras each year to reward the players for their efforts. There are many ways that a head coach can make a very average season special, and many student-athletes are as concerned with these many "extras" as they are with winning and losing.

The coach of a youth league team, even with very limited funding, can provide some extra rewards to his players. The idea of presenting a player with a game ball following a big win can serve as a reward to players as well as motivation to individuals in future contests. With the help of a local restaurant, a coach could set up a team meal for players after a big game. Even the idea of setting up a team event at a player's home to watch videotape of the team's latest game is a way to spend quality time with your players away from the court or game field.

The baseball facility I took over at my high school already had a grass infield complete with an irrigation system, brick in-ground dugouts, fenced in bullpens, and a press box/coaches' office behind home plate. Even though the facilities were excellent, I have still managed to make improvements. We have installed an 8 x 18 foot scoreboard, added windscreen to the outfield fence, put up new fair poles, added a stereo/public address system, and cemented and carpeted our outdoor batting tunnel. For the players, we purchased team jackets, team bags, and mesh batting practice jerseys. We have team training equipment such as a video camera to analyze player performance and a radar gun to chart pitchers' ball velocity. Beyond those "extras" we have made arrangements with several local restaurants to feed our players team meals. We also arranged an annual spring break trip to the Virginia Beach area to play nonconference games. While our team gets the benefit of playing three games in three days against very good competition, our players get the opportunity to bond with each other on the bus ride, as hotel roommates, and eating team meals together.

But the vast majority of sports programs don't have the funding and civic backing of our baseball program. Poorly funded or nonfunded programs, including youth leagues, can improve their situations through fundraising. The key to improving a team or league's financial status involves setting a financial goal, creating a plan, and getting players, coaches, and parents active in the community in an effort to raise monies needed for improvements. The types of fundraisers a team or league can initiate can range from leaguewide efforts such as selling advertising on the league facility to selling items to neighbors; types of fundraisers that can be run by individual teams include bake sales, car washes, or having local businesses sponsor each team. (Fundraising is covered in more detail in Chapter 8 and sample fundraising letters are in the appendix.)

One of the best ways to improve a program is always to be on the lookout for new ideas. Observing other coaches and their programs is a great resource. By learning what activities have been successful, you can make better decisions about how to upgrade your own team or program.

Learning from Other Coaches

I think that Paul Brown was, in my mind, the greatest innovator as a coach. Not that I'm an expert, but I've been around it a little bit.—Bill Belichick

One thing should be clear to all coaches—they don't know everything. Good coaches are always learning or "lifting" ideas from other coaches. This could range from borrowing ideas from coaches they played for to coaches they have competed against to strategies they have seen in college or professional games on television or in person. Good coaches constantly look for new ideas. Almost all the coaching methods, strategies, and philosophies that coaches use are something they learned from some other coach or leader.

An example of this can be found by analyzing the effect of professional basketball's influence upon college and high school basketball. In the 1980s, scoring in high school and college basketball games soared. This was no doubt due to the influence of Pat Riley's "Showtime" Lakers who had a knack for scoring on the fast break in bunches. In the mid-1990s, individual skills were stressed to young players as Michael Jordan (nearly) single-handedly took the Chicago Bulls to six NBA championship titles. The last few years, numerous college and high school teams have emphasized passing, cutting, and sharing the basketball due to the success of upstart teams such as the Sacramento Kings.

Go to Coaching Clinics

One of the best ways to get information and ideas from other coaches is to attend coaching clinics. If you are interested in learning from other coaches, regardless of what level you coach, there is a setting to hear and learn from other seasoned coaches. Simply by doing some research in your local paper, through your league's board of directors, or on the Internet, you can find the clinic that best suits your needs.

If you are new to coaching, you may want to go to a general coaching clinic. These clinics may instruct you on basic issues like how to develop a team goal, how to communicate with athletes and parents, how to run a practice, teaching sportsmanship, etc.

If you are coaching a more advanced group of athletes, then you will probably be better served by attending sport-specific clinics. For example, if you are dedicated to coaching only one sport, let's say, football, then you probably want to attend a clinic specifically for football coaches. A clinic like this usually breaks off into two main groups with speakers for offense and defense. Depending on what position you will be coaching, you would listen to the expert speaker in your specific area. Speakers could range from former players, longtime youth league coaches, high school or college coaches, or professional coaches.

The bottom line is that if you want to be a better coach for your athletes, regardless of your background, clinics are a great way to improve your coaching knowledge.

The following are a few hints at how to get the most from a clinic:

• Take a pen and paper and take notes.
• Sit in the front few rows.
• Learn at least one new thing.
• Ask questions.

Reflect on Coaches in Your Past

The best coaching models may be coaches you played for earlier in life. It can be extremely productive for you to compare the way you lead your team to that of the coaches you played for. Inevitably, coaches will most likely mirror much of the style, philosophy, and methods that their own coaches used to guide them years ago, but you should not try to imitate your old coach in every respect. In fact, a coach may use some methods that they know were effective when they played, while they may try new methods in other areas in an effort to be more effective with their own players today. Some coaches may also take inspiration from coaches in the past or famous coaches; that is OK, since most successful coaches at any level share the qualities of honesty, sportsmanship, hard work, and the ability to adapt and innovate. You may want to make a list of those qualities, practice plans, plays, and comments that made the most impression on you, that you admired, or that you think were effective.

The first coach in nearly every athlete's life is usually a parent. Either your father or mother, or maybe even both, showed you how to throw a ball or work with your first swing. I cannot overstate the importance of an athlete's parents in their career. The encouragement, support, and guidance of a parent is probably the biggest influence in a child's decision to compete in athletics.

Using myself as an example, both of my parents encouraged me early on, and throughout my playing career I had the opportunity to play for several exceptional coaches. The teaching of fundamentals and fun contests that Steve Welpott employed with my Little League teams are seen at the beginning and end of my practices. Wayne Todd, my high school baseball coach, was highly organized and I got the idea of using a practice plan from him as well as the role of strong discipline in running a team. Finally, Mike Lonergan, my basketball coach at Catholic University, convinced me that I could make a good program even better by taking on stiff competition and traveling each year to expose my players to bigger challenges in addition to other high school programs in our area. He also made me realize that even if you are relatively young, you can still run an effective sports program.

The idea is that if you are new to coaching and looking for a place to start on how to develop your coaching style, you may want to look at the positive qualities your own coaches employed in getting the most out of you and your teammates. After you gain more experience as a coach, you can develop your own philosophy and style depending on what works best for you and your athletes.

5

Head Coach and Assistant Coaches

Are you saying that the assistant had the answers all along, he just wasn't telling anyone?—Jim Valvano

In order to run a school athletic team or program, one person cannot do everything to a satisfactory level. Every coach needs competent assistant coaches or volunteers. Any school head coach who has achieved sustained success has had one or more assistant coaches who understand and execute their supporting role. Likewise, anyone who volunteers to coach a recreational league team finds additional assistance from other volunteers makes the difference between being able to coach effectively or not.

Using a youth football team as an example, try to picture how one head coach could possibly run a productive practice if he has to coach all the various positions—linemen, quarterback, running back, and wide receiver—and that is just covering the offense! During an offensive practice, at least three coaches are needed; one for the linemen, one for the quarterbacks, and one to teach the skill positions such as running back and receivers. On a day where the team stresses defensive practice, one coach could teach the linemen, another coach could teach the linebackers, and another could work with the secondary. Regardless of how much one coach knows, it is necessary to delegate teaching the various specialty positions of a sport to assistant coaches.

I have three assistants on my baseball staff. It would be difficult, if not impossible, for me to teach all the skills in each area to all of the players in our program. I normally focus on one or two areas to teach my players. Most years I will coach the pitchers and work with all the hitters in the program. That means that I assign the other major areas to my three assistant coaches. One assistant coach teaches the catchers, one works with the infielders, and one works with the outfielders.

In the preseason I meet several times with each of my assistants to discuss the various aspects of each position that I expect them to teach. For example, I will review with my outfield coach all the various skills and fundamentals that I want every outfielder in our program to master, such as the crow hop, fielding a routine ground ball, fielding a ball on the run, and catching a routine fly ball. Through these meetings I am confident that my outfielders will be taught the necessary skills to be a good outfielder at the high school level. I meet and discuss the same type of

Certain responsibilities are the head coach's alone, and assistant coaches need to respect the head coach's authority, but assistants, if wisely chosen, are oftentimes a head coach's most valuable resource. (BRHS)

details with my infield coach and my catching coach. By taking the time to work with my assistant coaches ahead of time, it allows me to focus on coaching the pitchers and hitters each day of practice.

Since most school programs allow for assistants, coaching staffs are readily assembled. But how can you, as a volunteer head coach for your daughter's youth league softball team, teach all the skills of the game without any help? You can't. Therefore you must enlist the assistance of other parent volunteers. Do not try to coach a team alone.

Imagine how efficient a softball practice would be if a head coach had two parents playing the role of assistant coaches during each practice. In one hour, the team which normally consists of twelve players could be broken into three groups of four players in each group. By having each of the three coaches run twenty-minute stations, players would have the opportunity to get many more repetitions in various skills. For example, station one could consist of four girls practicing fielding ground balls at shortstop and making throws to first base, station two could involve four girls practicing catching fly balls from different outfield locations and making throws to second base, and station three could consist of four girls alternating between hitting live pitching and hitting soft toss in the batting tunnel. Simply by getting two people to help run her practice, a head coach is able to have her players get a suitable number of practice repetitions fielding, throwing, and hitting softballs compared to the handful of chances they would get under one coach. The same setup can be adapted to soccer, hockey, or just about any team practice.

With a youth league team or park team there may be several parents who share the responsibility of "head" coach. In my opinion, even if several adults share the coaching responsibilities evenly during practices, one adult must assume the role of head coach on game night. This will eliminate confusion with players, parents, and game officials as to who is actually leading the team.

Probably the greatest misconception most spectators have about many sports teams is the amount of work done by a head coach on game night. In many cases, a head coach focuses primarily on one set of position players, while he oversees the overall performance of all the various positions on a team. If a head coach has competent assistants on his staff, then he can focus on one particular area and not get overloaded with the task of trying to critique and teach every player on the field or court during every game.

Another misconception about head coaches is that they are always the most knowledgeable member of the coaching staff. A smart head coach removes his ego from the equation and lets his assistant coaches teach to their strength (even if it is a position he would like to coach himself). Each of my assistants has helped me to be a better head coach. I have had three former Division I scholarship baseball players as my varsity assistant coaches. All three of these coaches had played different positions at the collegiate level—infielder, pitcher, and catcher. Each showed me the best way to coach players in the position of his specialty. This has allowed me to improve my teaching of those positions. Volunteer coaches may find that another parent whose child plays on the team may have sports experience that they can share with the team.

Head coaches and assistant coaches have many responsibilities and characteristics in common. First, all coaches are expected to be professional, passionate, and extremely dedicated. Regardless of their title, all coaches need to be prepared every day they work with their players, should have plenty of enthusiasm, and expect to put in long hours. Second, all coaches enjoy competition. Most coaches are typically former athletes who have a desire to pass on their knowledge and passion for sports and competition to younger players. Last, regardless of whether they are a head coach or assistant coach, all coaches want to see their players succeed. Whether they are a linebackers coach or a head softball coach, coaches want to see their athletes experience success.

Head coaches do understand, however, that there are certain specific responsibilities that fall squarely on their shoulders. The University of Texas head football coach, Mack Brown, has stated that the main difference between head coaches and assistant coaches is that "assistant coaches make suggestions, head coaches make decisions." The first, and for me, the worst, part of being a head coach is cutting players from a team. The head coach is ultimately responsible for deciding who is and who is not on a team. The head coach has the unenviable task of breaking the bad news to a hopeful athlete. This is a task that should never be delegated. Throughout the years that I have coached sports, cutting athletes is the only aspect of the job which I always dislike. There are, however many sports, such as football, wrestling, cross-country, and track that have flexibility in team size. At many schools these sports allow participation regardless of the athlete's ability level.

The second responsibility of being a head coach is what I call the "dirty work." These are the areas of coaching that include game decisions and those that extend far beyond the playing field on game night. A head coach usually decides sport specific items such as what skills will be taught in practice and how much playing time each player gets. Playing time, along with game strategies, are the two most visible areas of being a head coach because of the numerous spectators who judge the team's success on game night. Success and failure, in terms of wins and losses, is usually judged by who the coach decides to play and what game strategy the coach decides to employ. As a rule of thumb, a coach must be willing to step up and accept responsibility when the team comes up short, and he should be eager to praise his athletes when the team is successful. Beyond sports specific decisions, a head coach is usually in charge of monitoring players' grades, off season weight training and conditioning, scheduling, fundraising, improving facilities, ordering equipment, arranging transportation, and so on. These numerous, behind-the-scenes, duties often go unnoticed or unknown by players and parents, yet they go a very long way in the success a team has during the season.

A head coach always has to know that the assistant coaches on his staff will be loyal to him. When a head coach faces the normal adversity expected during just about any sports season, whether it is questioning himself following a tough loss or if it is a disgruntled player who is appealing to a member of the coaching staff about playing time, a head coach has to know that he and his entire staff are always on the same page. An assistant coach could be the most knowledgeable person in the world at coaching a particular sport, but if he shows up late to practices or games, disagrees with the head coach in front of the team, or teaches a skill or concept that does not fit in with the program philosophy, he is actually more of a burden than an asset. The word "assist" means to help, so an assistant coach's actions should do just that. Along those lines, assistant coaches can disagree with a head coach, but they have to support the coach on the field. An assistant coach should never openly question a head coach's philosophy, strategies, methods, or decisions in front of players. Players on a team follow the example that is set for them by the coaching staff, so if they see an assistant coach questioning or challenging a head coach, inevitably they will begin to do the same. This same principle applies to volunteer assistants who help a volunteer head coach.

What Makes a Quality Assistant Coach

One of the most important decisions you will make as a head coach is how to select quality assistant coaches. Finding assistant coaches that are dedicated, focused, knowledgeable, and trust-worthy is essential for your coaching success. This also goes for volunteer coaches who are seek-ing additional volunteer help.

When interviewing potential assistant coach-es, you should ask both sports-related and non-sports questions such as:

- Are you willing to learn the head coach's terminology, strategies, and philosophy?

- What kind of importance do you place on winning?

- How would you react to a player or parent who comes to you to discuss playing time?

- What kind of time commitment are you will-ing/able to make?

- What are your sport specific strengths?

- What are your sport specific weaknesses?

- How would you address a player who misbe-haves? Doesn't hustle? Skips practice?

The more you learn about a person's knowl-edge base, strategies, and people skills the better your chances of choosing the right person to fit your needs and the needs of the players in your program. From my own experience as a head coach, I firmly believe that my assistant coaches have taught me more about sports and working with young people than I have ever taught them.

Head coaches and assistant coaches need to have many of the same characteristics of all effective coaches. Certain responsibilities are the head coach's alone, and assistant coaches need to respect the head coach's authority. Assistant coaches, if wisely chosen, are often a head coach's most valuable resource.

6

Winning Isn't Everything

Winning isn't everything, but wanting to win is.
—Vince Lombardi

Amateur athletic competition should be used primarily as a tool for helping to develop the character of young people. The balancing act of teaching players to be extremely competitive in an effort to win games, while at the same time teaching the value of sportsmanship, is an area which all coaches constantly think about. If a coach's desire to win games ever begins to outweigh the ability to demonstrate and teach proper sportsmanship to athletes, that coach has failed to teach his athletes some important, lifelong lessons.

Effective coaches are primarily concerned with developing people. They stress the importance of handling winning and losing in a sportsmanlike manner. A player who learns the correct way to handle winning with class and losing with their head up will eventually become an adult who learns to place success and set backs in the proper perspective. If a player comes to practice the day following a big win and does not work hard, his coach can make him practice with the second team that day in order to send the message to the athlete that he must maintain a top-notch work ethic. This athlete won't forget that lesson in a hurry, and it may even stay with him for the rest of his life. Similarly, if a coach can teach an athlete to continue to persevere and work hard in an effort to bounce back after a tough loss, then the athlete learns how to handle constructively negative situations that he may face in the future. Effective coaches treat a loss as an opportunity to help their team members to determine what went wrong, figure out how to correct it, and help their players prepare better for future contests.

Coaches can use winning and losing as a teaching tool to reinforce positive traits and discourage negative traits which their individual athletes and teams may be demonstrating during games. Just by having your players write down three things that the team does well on the nights they win, or three areas where they struggle on the nights they get defeated, is a great way for athletes to learn how to analyze their play individually and as a team. For example, if a basketball team tells their coach that the nights they win they limit their turnovers, play good defense, and out rebound their opponent, then they have begun the process of understanding what it takes to be successful on game night. If the team identifies excessive turnovers, poor shooting, and lack of hustle as common mistakes they make when they lose a game, then they can begin to focus their efforts on improving in these areas to avoid future defeats. By having your athletes identify their strengths and weaknesses, you have taught your players a skill that will serve them well beyond their athletic careers.

A school's head coach can assume without being told by his athletic director or principal that he or she needs a reasonable amount of success in terms of wins and losses. That being said, in all my years of coaching, I have never had a principal or athletic director tell me that winning games was the key to keeping my job. In many cases, school administrators are far more concerned with the experience of the athletes and the views of their parents than with the number of games the team wins.

Sportsmanship

A coach should make sportsmanship a priority from day one with their coaches, players, and parents. A coach is responsible for teaching and demonstrating to his or her players the right way to handle winning and losing.

Any player or coach can demonstrate outstanding sportsmanship, respect for game officials, respect for teammates and opponents, and so on when things are going great for them individually or for the team. We tell the players in our baseball program that the true test of character takes place when individuals and teams face adversity, and that is when it is most important to remember to practice good sportsmanship.

Effective coaches know that their athletes will follow their lead in this area. If a football coach tells his players to ignore any call by a referee that they disagree with, but he spends the majority of his time and energy on Friday nights screaming at the officials, he is sending the wrong message to his athletes. If a coach decides to ignore or turn a blind eye to poor sportsmanship, he is reinforcing to his athletes that their poor behavior isn't as much of an issue as throwing strikes or making jump shots. The worst reason for a coach to avoid correcting unsportsmanlike behavior is to believe that a kid is such a competitor that he hates losing. Very few people who play or coach competitive sports like to lose, but being competitive does not excuse inappropriate behavior by coaches, players, or fans.

There can be many opportunities to reinforce a positive response or criticize a negative one. For instance, if a coach witnesses his team shaking hands with their opponents following a tough loss, he should applaud his players' efforts, and praise their maturity and class. If a coach witnesses poor sportsmanship, such as throwing equipment or finger pointing following a negative play, the coach must address the situation immediately. Waiting to discuss it until the next day, or in a

Teaching good sportsmanship is one of the chief goals of every great coach. (Bob Updegrove)

one-on-one setting is too late. By immediately identifying poor sportsmanship, communicating to players that it is unacceptable behavior, and demanding that the offender correct the problem, an effective coach teaches his players that the way they handle positive and negative situations is a high priority.

Teaching sportsmanship has always been part of coaching sports, but the need for it may be more urgent now than ever before. Consider the results of a survey of more than four thousand athletes conducted by the Character Counts! Coalition (see **Collegiate Baseball**, October 1, 2004).

• 58% of male athletes and 24% of female athletes think it is proper to deliberately inflict pain in football to intimidate an opponent.

• 47% of males and 19% of females think it is proper to "trash talk" a defender after a score.

- 27% of males and 21% of females think it is proper to soak a football field to slow down an opponent.

- 25% of males and 14% of females think it is proper to alter illegally a hockey stick.

If one-fourth to one-half of our athletes today step onto the court or field with these views, coaches need to make teaching sportsmanship a higher priority.

Important Games and Winning/Losing Streaks

Two areas which all coaches must learn to handle are: (1) winning and losing important games, and (2) winning streaks and losing streaks. Following a very important contest, say a game which determines whether or not a team will qualify for their postseason tournament, a coach must take the time to discuss with their team what they can learn from their efforts. If his team wins its big game, a coach may take the time to point out the important team concepts that led to a victory in this pressure-packed setting. He could point out that he is proud of their success because they worked hard to reach their goal of making the playoffs, they had sacrificed individual goals for the good of the team, and that their months of off-season training put them in this enviable situation. In contrast, if his team is on the losing side of an important game, an effective coach must use the event as a teaching opportunity. He might point out to his team that while he is proud of the effort that his players gave, they will have to reassess their team and individual goals and they must make changes to their off-season training routines to improve their chances for future success.

Having a winning or losing streak is either one of the best or one of the worst feelings you can experience as a head coach. When your team is winning night after night, you and your players may develop a certain confidence which borders on cockiness. You feel that the decisions you make as a coach will almost certainly work out for the best for your team, while your players feel that they can execute their fundamentals against even the toughest opponents. The opposite extreme is the desperation felt by coaches and players during a losing streak. When your team constantly comes up short on game night, you may question every decision you make with your athletes and game strategy, while your players struggle to maintain their focus on team goals.

My advice on how to handle winning and losing streaks is simple: remember that they are always one game away from ending. A team which feels it can't be beat runs the risk of becoming overconfident when several consecutive games have been won. An effective coach will point out to a team areas that they can still improve upon. If he doesn't do this, he is reinforcing the idea that as long as the team is winning everything is fine. A team which is facing a string of losses must be constantly reminded by their coach that they are not far away from turning things around and going in the right direction.

Participation, Skills, and Work Ethic

At the youth league or sub-varsity level, participation and skill development are usually stressed over winning and losing. This philosophy is absolutely appropriate for this age and playing level. As a junior varsity basketball coach, I know that my best freshmen or sophomore players may move up to the varsity team, which may significantly decrease my team's ability to win. My main goal as a JV coach is to prepare players for the rigors of competition on the varsity level. Whether my team wins fifteen games or five games is not nearly as important as to whether they master the fundamentals skills, work ethic, and understanding of teamwork needed for success at the next level.

Coaches would be surprised at how focusing on participation, skill development, and hard work can lead to team success without actually stressing winning with your athletes. I remember coaching an extremely young baseball team in a very competitive league where we were overmatched night after night by more experienced, talented teams. My coaching staff and I decided to focus less on our losing record and more on whether our players were playing the game to the best of their abilities. Then an interesting thing happened—the less that my staff and I harped on our players about winning and losing, the more our young team relaxed and began playing good baseball. Before we knew it, our team began winning games.

Coaches need to be more concerned with the process of playing good sports rather than the result of each game. This works for both wins and losses. If a team plays poorly but wins, you can stress the areas that need improvement to ensure better success in future games. If your team plays great but comes up short, you should make your players aware that you are pleased with their efforts. By focusing on playing the game the right way, instead of on the outcome of each contest, you are teaching your players that their preparation, their attitudes, and their ability to handle success and failure in athletic competition are what really matter.

Team Play

Coaches are always looking for players to fill certain roles on a team. In basketball, a player does not have to score twenty points per game to help his team win. Someone has to handle the ball, pass, and play defense. In baseball, not everyone hits home runs, so a player should learn to hit, bunt, run the bases, and play defense. Not everyone is going to be a star, therefore if a player is willing to fill important yet less glamorous roles, that player increases his chances of playing and enhances the team's chances of success.

Like many coaches, I have always stressed to my players that all members of a team are equal. It is important to spell out clearly for athletes what their role on a team is. Obviously, roles can change due to injury or players improving their abilities, but you don't want to mislead players about what they need to do for your team to be successful. You should do your best to judge all players on level ground. If a player, no matter what his or her role, is not executing or following established team rules about practice, behavior, or hustle, then there should be consequences, whether it is loss of playing time or extra conditioning. You should be aware that all members of a team need to feel that they are valuable to the team. If a player comes off the bench and makes a big shot or gets a big hit, it is good to praise that athlete's accomplishment in front of his teammates as a reward for his patience, effort, and contribution to the team's success.

Youth Leagues

Coaches need to balance the natural desire to win with the need to make practice and games fun for the players. Youth leagues are one place where winning matters least, but where a demoralizing experience can turn off a young player to sports

An effective coach makes each player feel valuable to the team and teaches them how to perform as a unit. (Bob Updegrove)

for good. Very few youth league athletes actually continue playing sports as teenagers. Many blame burnout, while others point the finger at coaches and parents who are too intense or demanding. I believe that the one factor that contributes to numerous athletes becoming discouraged and quitting before they are given a chance to develop their talent is sitting on the bench. I was always taught that the point of playing Little League sports was to let kids have fun. Well, if a seven-year-old player spends the majority of a Little League contest standing on the sidelines because his coach's main priority is winning the league championship, the overlooked athlete will probably find better ways to spend his time next season. Coaches of six- to twelve-year-olds need to recognize that winning the Little League championship is not as important as giving all the players on the team the opportunity to get a hit, shoot a basket, or make a tackle. I make the specific point when I speak at any Little League or AAU clinic that I never consider a young athlete's performance record. What I do watch for are character traits such as attitude, hustle, respect for teammates, opponents, and game officials. And I am not alone in this. By stressing this point to youth league coaches, I hope to reinforce the fact that winning at the youth league or sub-varsity levels is secondary to the qualities an athlete can develop at a young age that will eventually lead him to success at the high school level and beyond.

If athletes are taught at a young age the importance of fair play and proper behavior, then they will be classy winners, gracious losers, and mature competitors throughout their sports and school years and perhaps for the rest of their lives.

7

Handling Difficult Situations

Remember this, the choices you make in life, make you.
—John Wooden

Whether you are a brand new volunteer coach or a head coach with decades of experience, you can count on conflicts arising during the course of the season. Besides the normal duties such as preparing for opponents, getting players to and from games on time, and making strategic game decisions, a coach may encounter any number of difficult situations such as: cutting athletes or removing an athlete from his team, handling problem behaviors outside of sports, communicating with unhappy parents, dealing with difficult referees or umpires, coaching your own child, managing anger, or handling personality conflicts and dissension within a team. This chapter offers specific suggestions and advice on how to address difficult situations you may face during your coaching experience.

Cutting and Dismissing Players

Two events that no coach enjoys are cutting or dismissing athletes from your team. The unfortunate reality is there are only so many spots available on any given team, which means that a coach has the dubious honor of selecting who gets to be part of the team and who does not. Depending on your league or school philosophy, you may carry only enough members on your team to be able to scrimmage and practice effectively; or you may be in the situation where you can carry extra players who primarily serve as practice players. By carrying a limited amount of players, a coach runs the risk of not having enough players available when sickness or injury sidelines a team member during a season. On the other hand, if a team has too many players it is nearly impossible for the players to get the necessary practice repetitions and game time to make their season worthwhile. These are some of the factors a coach must consider when he determines how many players he will carry on each year's team.

As to the process of cutting an athlete from the team during the tryout period, I believe that this should be done in a one-on-one setting. I firmly believe that if an athlete has spent several days doing everything he can to prove he belongs on your team for a season, the least the coach can do is sit down, look that athlete in the eye, and tell him why he was not selected for the team. A word of caution: choose your words very carefully when you explain to an athlete why he did not make your team. If, when you speak with the athlete, you describe his tryout performance in a negative manner, you may be eliminating any chance that the athlete will be willing to try again or even participate in that sport in the future. In a one-on-one conversation, it is best to tell an athlete what you saw during the tryout period that you viewed as a positive and any areas where improvement was needed. Hopefully, this leaves the athlete with a feeling that he has certain strengths that he can build upon while he works on areas of weakness. With this approach, he can feel that he can be prepared to try again next year.

In developmental leagues where there are many players on a team, it is worth a coach's time to explain to players and parents alike that all players will get the opportunity to play in games. By making it clear to everyone ahead of time that the goal of the team and league is to help players improve, a coach can help to avoid numerous problems with players and parents who may otherwise get upset when a weaker player's involvement in a game may hurt the team's chances for winning.

Dismissing athletes from your team is much more serious. Every coach must understand and comply with the school or league policies regarding excluding an athlete from participation. This will avoid the awkward and embarrassing situation of a coach dismissing a player and subsequently learning that his action was contrary to school or league policy. Unfortunately, after a coach has explained team rules about conduct or effort to players and parents, a player's repeated disregard for proper behavior may force a coach to make the difficult decision to remove a player from his team.

Several things need to be kept in mind when dismissing a player from your team:

• Make sure your decision is in accordance with school or league policy.

• Tell your athlete and his parents the reason(s) why the athlete is being removed from the team.

• Document the specific dates and times of any instances of misconduct that led to your decision.

• Keep your league or school administrators informed of these situations as they develop. Your league president or school principal does not want to learn about this from an irate parent or be unprepared to address the situation.

The unfortunate instance of having to dismiss a player from a team is another reason why is it essential to have your team rules signed by your players and their parents before the season starts. By listing both the rules and the consequences of not following them, you eliminate any "gray area" regarding the penalties for rule infractions. For example, you might state on your team rules a specific set of consequences such as: "Breaking a team rule once will lead to a one-on-one conference with your parents, a second infraction will lead to a one-game suspension from the team, and a third infraction of team rules would lead to dismissal from the team."

If you happen to coach in a youth league that does not have a written set of rules or code of conduct for players, then you may want to create a basic set of rules to govern conduct and present them to your league board of directors for approval. Depending on their reaction to your suggestion, you might offer to have these rules serve as guidelines for behavior for all the players in the league. If your suggestion is met with a mixed reaction, then you may want to ask to use the rules with your own team and then reevaluate their effectiveness with the board at the conclusion of the season.

Players with Problems Outside of Sports

At some point during your coaching career, you will have to deal with an athlete who has personal problems they bring to the athletic arena. These may include problems with honesty or being a good teammate, substance abuse, problems with the law, or family conflicts. Depending on the severity of these cases a coach must handle these situations and ask himself if he is willing to make decisions that are in the best interest of the athlete as well as his team.

When dealing with a player who brings character flaws to the team setting, a coach has to determine the best way to handle this individual. For example, let's say that a coach learns that a player has been dishonest with teammates or the coaching staff or that the athlete has displayed a selfish attitude since he made the team. There are several ways that a coach could handle the situation. First, he could choose to ignore the behavior. The problem with this lack of action, of course, is that the negative behavior would most likely continue throughout the year, and other players on the team may start to display these same negative characteristics. The second way a coach could handle the situation could involve dismissing the player from the team. The problem with this type of severe decision is that the coach has not given the player a chance to alter their behavior.

The third and best way to handle a situation like this is to have a one-on-one conversation with the player. As uncomfortable as it may be, a coach needs to address the negative behavior with the athlete as soon as the coach becomes aware of it. The coach needs to state that a change in the athlete's behavior is expected, and he must be clear that if a definite and consistent change is not made there will be specific consequences. I strongly suggest documenting the date and general ideas exchanged in this discussion in case problems continue with this athlete that may lead to major consequences. For example, if a player displays a selfish attitude in the future he will have to face the consequences, ranging from extra conditioning to suspension from the team.

If a coach is faced with a player on his team who has made poor choices in his personal life such as experimenting with illegal drugs or getting into trouble with the law, he must do what is best for the athlete. Although the athlete usually does not want to be removed from the team, a coach must make that decision so the athlete can focus their time and energy on getting their personal life in order. A coach's decision may even be required by school or league policy which precludes participation on teams for those who engage in any illegal activity.

Young athletes who are experimenting with illegal substances or find themselves in trouble with the law need more help than a sports coach can offer. Young people who are taking drugs—and this includes steroids and other drugs used to enhance performance or energy—should enter some type of treatment program or counseling so they can begin to understand the negative effects that these decisions have on their body and mind now and in the future. As for athletes who find themselves in trouble with the law, I fall back on my father's philosophy that getting to participate in activities like sports is a privilege, not a right. Athletes who make poor moral choices that lead them to criminal behavior should not be on a sports team with student-athletes who make an honest effort in school, are respectful of their teachers and parents, and care about their teammates. Allowing athletes who make these types of destructive decisions to remain on a team is a disservice to the troubled athlete who should be focusing on improving their personal life away from sports. Additionally, it is not fair to allow these athletes the privilege of competing side by side with the overwhelming number of student-athletes who maintain the high standard of behavior that effective coaches demand.

If a coach notices a player who is making destructive decisions that he may attribute to situations beyond the athlete's control, such as a child who one believes is being abused or neglected, then the coach has an obligation to contact public service or health officials to determine if the athlete is in an unsafe situation at home. As difficult as it is to deal with, a coach must understand that an athlete may occasionally act irrationally because of a difficult circumstance he cannot control. If that is the case, removing that athlete from the team may be cutting him off from the support he desperately needs most at that moment.

In helping athletes to deal with difficult circumstances in their personal lives, a coach must determine how much help he can truly offer to a child in need. My baseball staff and I have an "open-door policy" which has been used by numerous athletes over the years. We have had players come to us for help with academics. Other players have come to us to discuss social problems. The most severe example that I can recall involved an athlete informing me that he was trying to convince a relative to seek treatment for an addiction.

The best advice that I can offer to you when giving guidance to young people is to use your best judgment, but realize that your ideas profoundly influence your athletes' decisions on how to handle their situations. If you feel unqualified to answer difficult questions for your athletes, or if you notice a significant change in an athlete's behavior, then make sure to contact the appropriate parties needed to help resolve the current issues. This may mean setting up a conference with the athlete's guidance counselor at school or making a phone call home to make sure that the athlete's parents are fully aware of the situation.

Unhappy Parents

Another difficult situation is dealing with unhappy parents. The issue which most frequently upsets parents and players is playing time. I will offer several pieces of advice that a coach can use to reach an understanding with parents on this matter.

First and foremost, never make promises to an athlete or his parents regarding playing time. Even if an athlete begins the year as your best hitter, shooter, or tackler, there is no guarantee that this will be the case by midseason or by the end of the year. Many factors can affect how your best player's season progresses. An athlete may become complacent with his performance or suffer injuries. Progress made by teammates throughout the season can easily change the status of certain players from full-time starters to being part of a platoon system. You can honestly communicate this point to the parents. Simply remind them of your policy of no guaranteed playing time which was made clear to everyone at the beginning of the season.

Second, when discussing playing time with parents, a coach should never discuss other athletes on the team with the athlete's parents. The moment a conversation goes down the road of, "We think Steve is a better player than David. We think he should play more than David . . . ." the coach is obligated to stop the conversation immediately. He should reiterate the policy to the parents that during a conversation about their son the topic should remain just that—about their son. A coach should feel comfortable discussing with an athlete's parents their child's strengths and weaknesses, but any attempt by a parent to try to improve their child's athletic standing by negatively describing the efforts of any athlete who is ahead of their child on the depth chart should be discouraged.

Third, I would tell any coach to stick by your guns. If a coach alters his lineup or playing rotation in an effort to please unhappy parents, then he will surely lose credibility with players (rightly so), while opening the door for every parent after every game to state their case for their son's need for increased playing time. A parent has the right to tell you they are not happy with their son's playing time; a coach has the responsibility to make the decision that he feels gives his team the best possible chance to be successful. This usually involves playing the athletes that he feels are the best on his team most often.

A conversation regarding playing time between a parent and coach may sound something like this:

"Hello, Coach Cassidy. This is Mrs. Smith."

"Hello, Mrs. Smith. How are you doing?"

"Well, okay, I guess, but I wanted to speak to you about Mike's playing time this year."

"Sure, what would you like to know?"

"Well, he has only played in five of the eight games the team has played this season."

"Yes, well right now Mike is our backup third baseman. I think he has done great with the opportunities I have given him this year."

"Well, I think that is the problem. I don't understand why he isn't getting more chances to play in games."

"To be honest with you, Mrs. Smith, Mike is a good hitter, but he needs to improve his fielding ability and arm strength to be a starter and these are areas that Mike and I have discussed as goals for his improvement this year. I know that he is working hard. If he continues to improve he may earn the opportunity to play more in games."

"Well, okay. I just don't want to see him get frustrated by not getting the chance to play as much as he would like to."

"Mrs. Smith, my staff and I have been working closely with Mike and he understands his role on the team at the moment. We will continue to work with him to help him improve and have a chance to earn more playing time."

"Thanks. I appreciate your attention to Mike. I just wanted to express my concerns."

"Thanks for calling, Mrs. Smith. If you have any other questions or concerns please do not hesitate to call me."

A simple two- or three-minute conversation such as this one can help coaches, players, and parents avoid the speculation and frustration that can often occur when coaches and parents don't talk. While the coach and parent in this particular situation didn't necessarily agree as to the player's role on this year's team, at least the player and parent will know what will be necessary for an increase in the athlete's playing time.

From my own experience as a player and as a coach, I always felt the coaches at a high school level were playing their best players in order to give their team a chance to win. Unhappy parents do not always feel this is the case. I have heard parents state that a particular coach does not play their son because "He doesn't like him," or "He plays favorites," or "He only plays seniors." The only answer I have for this is that no parent (and I am a parent myself) wants to admit that another player may be more talented than their son or daughter. It's not only the athlete's ego involved in sports today. If the parents of an athlete have been telling everyone who will listen that their son is the best player on the team, but that athlete repeatedly sits the bench, there is a good chance these parents will eventually come to the coach to vent their frustrations. If you try to speak with the parents and explain your reasoning for your decision, there is a good chance that they will disagree with you (which is their right). While parents want the coach to make a decision strictly to make themselves and their son happy, a coach must make the decision that is best for his team.

If a parent tries to question play selection or coaching style openly, a coach has to decide how to best handle the situation. A volunteer coach of a youth league team can normally make it clear to anyone who offers their advice that if they want to volunteer their personal time and energy to coach the team on game night they are more than welcome. All they have to do is be at practice everyday for two hours, five days a week, and then they can offer any advice they want to that will help the kids. This normally gets the point across to the advice-giver that if one feels the need to coach the team on game night, then you won't mind making a full-time commitment to the team and the kids.

With paid coaches at the school level, such as a junior high school or high school team, a coach can normally tell the parent that they are free to offer advice on how best to run the team. They should also make it clear to the parent that the school's athletic director or principal hired them to coach the team, so if they have any other ideas they should offer them to the school administration. A coach should be willing to hear any parent's concerns, but keep in mind that it is the coach, not the parents, who ultimately have the responsibility for how the team performs on game night. Therefore, a coach can not cloud his judgment with the numerous bits and pieces of advice that he gets from any source; he simply must decide what is best for his team and execute his plan on that basis.

Officiating

Another area with potential for difficulty, particularly for players and for young or inexperienced coaches, is the way they communicate and react to game officials. Many coaches feel that by voicing their displeasure over calls that go against their team they are fighting for their players. In most cases, they are probably doing more harm than good.

If an umpire or referee makes a call with which I disagree, I will politely let him know that I feel the call was incorrect and leave it at that. An effective coach understands that there is a way to speak to a referee or official that allows him to make his feelings known without making a bad situation worse.

Early in my coaching career I would constantly go onto the field to argue with umpires and call referees over to the basketball sideline so I could voice my displeasure with their decisions. I would usually do this immediately following the play that went against my team, so I would yell at the official instead of speaking with him. We've all seen this kind of display at all levels of sports. After several years of coaching I realized that not only did my action with officials and umpires not help my team; it was actually hurting my team's chances for success. It seemed like the more critical I was of an official's decision, the more calls went against my team for the remainder of each game. This was a referee's or umpire's way of telling me that I needed to be less confrontational when voicing my displeasure with their decisions.

What I usually do now when I disagree with an official's judgment is wait to speak to the umpire or official, in a normal tone of voice, at the next break in play. For example, if I believe one of my basketball players is being fouled by his opponent, I might ask the referee during a foul shot if he would watch the opposing players to make sure they are not holding my guys on offense. As a young coach, I would have simply screamed at the referee during the action to "Call the foul!" I am now getting my message across to the referee, but in a more respectful tone and at a better time. On the baseball diamond, I wait until the end of an inning to talk with the umpire regarding his decisions. Again, a coach who talks to an umpire during a break in the action stands a much better chance of being heard and getting a more thoughtful explanation.

Because knowing when and how to dispute a call takes maturity and judgment, I believe it is best left to the coach. When it comes to players talking to the officials about the calls they make, I simply tell my athletes: "Don't." A referee or umpire has to hear criticism from the spectators on nearly every call they make. They have to put up with it. They do not have to put up with a fifteen-year-old who uses poor body language or has a critical comment following a call with which they disagree. They may even remove my player from the game. I will go on to ask my players, "When you have been critical of officials' decisions, what happens on the next close play?" Usually a few players will raise their hand and say, "The next close call goes against our team!"

As part of their duties, coaches teach their athletes to respect officials, opposing players, and others. (BRHS)

Why? Officials are human. They make mistakes just like every coach and player on the field. But if every time they make a call that goes against your team a player reacts poorly, you can be assured that it will not be the last time that a call goes against your team that night. Players who are disciplined enough to react well to adversity will usually help their team get the next close call to go in their favor, but teams full of players who complain or whine when an official's decision goes against them earn a reputation that will work against them throughout the game, and possibly, throughout the season. An umpire or referee will not change his decision because a player or coach disagrees, but a coach's or player's poor reaction to an official's decision can cause a player or his team to lose their composure, which can lead to defeat. Coaches and players need to keep this in mind the next time a call by an official doesn't go their way.

Coaching Your Own Child

Another circumstance which many coaches often find difficult to handle is coaching their own son's or daughter's team. If you decide to coach your own child, and are not careful about your decisions, you could make for a difficult season for everyone involved including your child, yourself, and other players and parents.

The first thing a parent who coaches their child must understand is that there may be a negative reaction from others regarding the situation. Does this mean a parent should not coach a team with their own child on it? Absolutely not. If a parent is willing to offer his time and energy to help all the members of a team, then he should be allowed to coach his child like he would any other player on the team.

Still, another player or parent from the team may say that a player receives an unfair advantage because their parent is a coach. The only way to counteract this is to treat your child the same way you would any player on your team. But don't go to the other extreme and ignore your child or be unfairly hard. The important point is to avoid drawing undue attention to the fact that your child plays on your team. If your daughter is the best hitter on the softball team then place her in the leadoff spot in your lineup; if she is not, don't. A parent who coaches needs to analyze objectively their child's athletic weaknesses like he would any other player on the team. If your son has not thrown strikes consistently in his last two pitching outings, then it is not fair to your team, or your son, for that matter, to have him pitch in the team's big game.

Perhaps the best reason a parent is obligated to treat his son or daughter the same as any other player on the field is that otherwise the child's transition to playing for another coach in the future will be extremely difficult. For example, if a parent of a youth league player is biased toward his son, he is setting his son up for a major disappointment when he plays for other coaches in the future who view this player's talents in an objective manner. The child who has always been the star player of the team when playing for his parent may have major problems adjusting to being treated like a regular player on the team. An effective coach treats all his players the same; even if the player is his own child.

Managing Anger

In terms of game behavior, I instruct all my athletes that there are plenty of coaches, fans, and parents who criticize referees or umpires, but the only job of an athlete is to play as hard and as well as they can. No matter how stern a warning a coach offers his team ahead of time, it is rare that all the players on a team will react to a bad call or other negative experiences with restraint throughout the entire year.

The best advice I can offer a coach on how to deal with an athlete's angry outbursts is to deal with it immediately, regardless of the game situation. The first time a basketball player argues with a game official or a baseball player throws his helmet or bat in disgust, a coach should immediately remove the player from the game. At the first break in the action, he should make it clear to the player that he has been removed because of his poor behavior, and that if the behavior is repeated at any point in the future then the consequences will be more severe (such as a suspension). By doing so, the coach sends the message to every athlete on the team that conducting oneself in a sportsmanlike manner takes precedence over winning the big game.

Arguing with officials distracts athletes from their ultimate goal of being successful on the playing field, it reflects poorly on the athlete himself, his teammates, his coaches, his school, and his family. Beyond that, I ask my players if they honestly think arguing with a referee or umpire makes things better for themselves and their teammates. Ultimately, when a young athlete argues with or tries to embarrass a game official, he hurts his team's chances for success in the long run, since most umpires or referees make questionable calls that go against a disrespectful team throughout a game.

Coaches, too, have to learn to control their anger when coaching. Players who do not play within the team concept or game officials who make calls which consistently go against that coach's team can lead to natural emotions ranging from frustration to anger. The bottom line is that coaches, like players, have to control their reactions when dealing with any adverse game situation. I often tell my players, "I would love to spend all my time yelling at the umpires or officials, but then I wouldn't be doing something. . . ." What I wouldn't be doing is coaching my players. Beyond that, I would lose my voice if all I ever did was scream at my players every time one of them makes a mistake. Simply put, there is a time, place, and manner to communicate how you feel to your players and game officials. You may be angry when a referee makes a bad call, but screaming at him from the coach's box does not improve your situation.

Talking to the referee during a break in the action, when you have calmed down, gives you a much better chance to get your point across to the official effectively. If all you do is bark at your players, then they will probably be too afraid or tentative to play their best. You are well within your bounds to let your players know you are unhappy with their efforts or their execution of the game plan; just make sure that you are telling them about your displeasure instead of lashing out at them in anger.

Personality Conflicts

Great coaches have a way of getting players of varying athletic levels and personalities to work together toward a common goal. Consider that as a head coach you may have a team made up of players who have different athletic experiences, come from different economic situations, different cultures, and have different personalities.

Effective coaches are able to get their players and teams to realize that when they are part of a team that they must be willing to sacrifice or alter their personal expectations and goals for the good of the team. For instance, if a basketball coach can explain to her best three scorers that the team will be better off if all three players share the ball equally, she will be able to avoid conflicts that may arise when all three players want to earn their status as the star of the team. If a football coach feels that his offense and defense are not getting along because one group is constantly blaming the other for the team's lackluster performance on game night, then he must communicate to the team that they are only as good as their weakest link. Therefore, if one group is struggling the problem is certainly not solved by bickering. If the team truly wants to succeed, they need to support each other's efforts to realize the goal they both share—winning on game night.

If a coach and a player have a personality conflict, then a one-on-one conversation usually is the best way to clear the air. For instance, if a player has been displaying poor body language when receiving constructive criticism from a coach, the coach may tell the player to see him after practice. The coach may start off the conversation by asking the player why he thinks the coach had him stay after practice. If the player does not understand why, then the coach should make it clear to the athlete that he disapproves of the athlete's reaction to receiving constructive criticism. The athlete may offer his side of events to the coach stating that he feels as if he is always being picked on or told what he should be doing differently. The coach needs to make it clear to the player that any advice a coach offers to a player is for one reason only—to help the player improve. Instructing a player on how to improve is not a personal attack on the player; it is simply the coach's way of communicating what the player needs to improve upon for his success, and the success of the team. He should also explain to the player that if he cannot receive advice from a coach, then he runs the risk of having coaches not offer advice to the player due to the fear that it will lead to future conflict. The problem with this hands-off approach is that the coach is allowing the player to accept that he does not need to improve. This is a disservice to the player and, in turn, to the whole team.

A coach needs to make sure that he and all his players are on the same page. If not, a team's self destruction is not just possible; it is highly probable.

Coaches show their true mettle in difficult situations. Cutting or removing players from the team, dealing with unhappy parents, handling questionable officiating, coaching your own child, and managing anger are all common challenges to the profession. Effective coaches understand that they must learn how to address these issues with consistency and poise and that these challenges are part of what any coach may face while leading a team through a successful season.

8

Running an Athletic Program

The will to win is important, but the will to prepare is vital.
—Joe Paterno

An athletic program consists of all the various non-game day tasks that surround the proper running of an athletic team or league, such as caring for equipment and facilities, running tryouts, scheduling games—even fundraising. Coaches spend an enormous number of hours working on their programs so that their teams can look, act, and play their best on game day, and players and coaches can focus on the most important and enjoyable part of sports—playing and coaching.

This chapter covers topics that any head coach should consider when setting up a successful athletic program. Some topics may not apply to the age or skill level of the young people you are coaching, but thinking about these topics will help you keep in mind the "big picture" that distinguishes the best athletic programs.

Tryouts

There are several schools of thought on how to run tryouts. At the youth level, tryouts are normally held to allow coaches to see and judge the experience and talents of all the players in a league in an effort to distribute them evenly to achieve the best parity among the teams and assure competitive games.

With AAU, junior high, or high school tryouts, I am aware of different theories about how to run a tryout. My first suggestion is to make your tryout as varied as possible. You should try to see as many aspects of a player's individual skills and talents as possible in the three or five day tryout period. By combining drills and intrasquad situations, a coach running a tryout can judge players on their individual skills, their ability to understand and accept coaching, and their ability to perform in game situations.

You should also make sure that you enter a tryout situation with an open mind. If a player who was cut from last year's team worked hard over the off-season and improves to the point where he is good enough to make this year's team, then you should reward that player's efforts. I once cut an athlete from our baseball program as a freshman. He went on to make our junior varsity team as a sophomore, our varsity as a junior, and was the captain of our team as a senior.

Remember that if you feel that you are unable to break the news to a young person that they have been cut from a team, there are plenty of recreational and instructional leagues that need quality coaches as well. Just understand that at the more competitive levels of athletics, cuts are necessary to make sure that teams have a manageable number of good players which will assure them to be competitive.

Scheduling

Every athletic team is different, so blanket statements such as, "I always schedule tough games early in our season," or "I want to schedule teams who we know we will beat every time," make very little sense to me.

If you have the opportunity to schedule your own opponents then you should avoid the two extremes: filling your schedule with too many strong teams or too many weak teams. In general, scheduling unbeatable competition leads to losses early in the season that can ruin your players' confidence. Scheduling very weak teams, on the other hand, can lead your team to have a false sense of confidence because the wins against these teams rarely serve as a good indicator of your team's strengths and weaknesses. Many youth or recreational teams do have to find all their opponents each season, however most schools and many league teams have regular conference or league games, so this self-scheduling would apply to nonleague or nonconference games.

If possible, you should alter your schedule yearly to meet the makeup of your particular team. This isn't always possible since some schedules are determined several years in advance, but good coaches always try to have a sense of what their team may look like several seasons in the future. If you have a team of talented, experienced players you may very well want to schedule the best competition you can find to challenge your team's ability. If you have a young or inexperienced team, it probably would be wiser to schedule less competitive teams to give your squad a fair chance at experiencing success. If you don't schedule to match the competitiveness of your young team, it could be the beginning of a very long year for the players and coaches of an over-matched team. Your overall goal when scheduling shouldn't be easy wins or overwhelming defeats; try to play opponents that will evenly match your team each season. This keeps the playing field level and results in a more positive experience for everyone.

Feeder Programs

Effective coaches work very closely with the coaches and, if possible, the players in their feeder programs. A feeder program is basically whatever level of play precedes the level in which a coach is currently coaching. For instance, a junior high football coach should work closely with the

Leading a team on game day is the most public aspect of coaching but it is just one of the many parts of an athletic program that an effective coach oversees. (BRHS)

youth league football coaches who will teach his future players basic fundamentals of football. In turn, the high school football coach should work closely with the junior high football coach to develop a common philosophy on how to best coach their players. The more time and energy that a coach spends teaching coaches and players in his feeder system, the more prepared his future players will be when they enter his program. By hosting or speaking at a coaching clinic, a school coach can clearly communicate what he desires in players with whom he will work as they move up through the youth league program.

There are other positive ways besides instruction that a coach can influence players in his feeder system. One way a coach can show his interest in young players is simply by going to a game or practice to observe the players in action. Another way a coach can encourage young players to take an interest in his program is by having a "League Night" where players are invited guests to a game so they get a first-hand look at players at the next level. Some coaches hold summer camps so young players can use the school's facilities and have the opportunity to work with the players and coaches at the school. The more interest that a coach shows in the players in his feeder league, the better the chances that he will generate the excitement needed to encourage future participation in that sport.

Weight Training and Conditioning

It is important to make sure that your players have or develop the necessary physical skills it takes to be safe and successful during games. One important concept about weight programs that new coaches need to understand is that, depending on your sport, programs which stress "bulking up" are exactly the opposite of what you want to preach to your players.

The first thing that coaches and athletes need to understand to train their bodies correctly is that getting bigger, in most cases, should not be the goal of most young athletes in training. Training can make an athlete stronger, quicker, and more flexible. Aside from the obvious advantages players gain for athletic success, the most important benefit of strength training is that the players on your teams will greatly reduce their chances for injury during athletic competition. This does not require heavy weight lifting. Coaches should know that most young athletes' bodies, which are still developing and growing, are not ready to handle the stress that heavy weight lifting places on their bodies. The rule of thumb I was always taught is that an athlete is ready for weightlifting when there is "hair on the chin." Typically, when a young man is ready to begin shaving, which is usually about age fourteen, his body has begun to grow so he can handle the physical rigors of heavier lifting. To be sure an athlete is ready to begin any weight training program, a young athlete and his or her parents should first consult with their doctor.

If a doctor tells a young athlete, parent, or coach that a young athlete's body is not ready for the weight room, there are still other ways to improve that athlete's strength and conditioning. The philosophy of an athlete "working against his own weight" means that he can do exercises such as push-ups, sit-ups, and dips to improve his overall strength. Young athletes can improve their speed by running wind sprints or taking a long jog several times weekly. Overall quickness and stamina can be addressed by having an athlete jump rope several minutes each day. Here is a sample workout program that involves no weights.

- Day 1: Jump rope for 3 minutes + 35 sit-ups
- Day 2: Five 50-yard sprints + 3 sets of 8 push-ups
- Day 3: 12-minute jog
- Day 4: Jump rope for 3 minutes + 3 sets of 5 dips
- Day 5: 3 sets of 8 push-ups + 35 sit-ups
- Day 6: 12-minute jog or eight 50-yard sprints
- Day 7: Day off

An effective coach recognizes several things about a program like this one. First, the program is balanced; it doesn't focus strictly on strength or quickness. Rather it will help an athlete with quickness, strength, speed, and endurance. Second, this program will not take long to perform each day, ten to twelve minutes in most cases. A third benefit of a program such as this one is that it is easy to improve your athlete's strength, speed, quickness, or endurance by simply adding a few more repetitions to each set of sit-ups or push-ups, or by adding a few more sprints or lengthening the jog by a few minutes. By following a non-weight lifting/conditioning program such as this one, your athletes will surely improve their chances for success on the athletic courts or fields, while reducing their chances of being seriously injured during practices or games.

For coaches at the junior high or high school levels whose athletes are old enough, and can make larger gains by participating in a training program that includes weight lifting, it is important to research what type of lifting best suits your athletes. A high school baseball coach will most likely emphasize an entirely different system of weight training from the high school football coach or a basketball coach. Coaches should decide if they want their players to participate in a general weight lifting program consisting of different exercises at varying weights and repetitions or to participate in a sport-specific weight lifting program that targets exercises to enhance sport-specific movements.

Regardless of the type of strength training a coach promotes, he should always ensure that his athletes lift weights with the supervision of a spotter. A spotter ensures that repetitions are being performed safely and correctly. The spotter's most important job involves helping fatigued athletes complete exercises in a safe manner. Never allow your athletes to lift weights by themselves.

Effective coaches understand that many younger athletes who are weight lifting for the first time may need to participate in a general weight lifting program designed to strengthen all the major areas of the body. A general program may include exercises designed to strengthen the neck, shoulders, chest, back, biceps, triceps, abdomen muscles, quadriceps, hamstrings, and calf muscles. Since such a wide variety of muscles have to be developed in young athletes, the best way to do this may be through a general strength training program where an athlete performs one exercise designed to build muscle in each of these areas. A standard exercise may include lifting a light weight from ten to fifteen repetitions.

A weight lifting program will vary according to your particular sport. It is the coach's responsibility to research the various programs of weight lifting that will best fit the needs of his athletes. For example, an effective baseball coach understands that his athletes don't need to get bulky to improve their overall baseball talent. While using heavy weights to develop certain parts of their bodies, many pitchers lift five- or ten-pound weights in a series of exercises known as "Jobes" that are meant to prevent injuries to a player's rotator cuff (an area essential for throwing a baseball). Therefore, it makes no sense for a high school baseball coach to have his players performing the same exercises at the same weights as a high school defensive tackle on the football team.

Effective coaches understand that they are not fitness professionals. The best advice that I can offer any coach is to do your homework. Educate yourself fully before implementing any type of strength or conditioning program with your athletes. If you don't, you may very well be doing your athletes and team more harm than good.

Related to the idea that weight lifting can be harmful for athletes, another practice for strength improvement has reared its ugly head more frequently in recent years. The desire to earn college scholarships which could lead to multimillion dollar professional contracts has become a borderline obsession for many young athletes. Some have decided to use body-enhancing drugs such as steroids to increase their physical gains. While the short-term effects of these drugs can often seem like a large advantage to teenage athletes attempting to gain the attention of college recruiters, coaches must make their athletes aware that the harmful and dangerous side effects of using these powerful drugs over the remainder of their lives far outweigh the limited benefits.

Besides causing physical damage or leading to serious illness, using drugs like steroids has been known to cause athletes to experience what is known as "roid rage." This involves bouts of depression mixed with violent outbursts of anger as the body attempts to adjust to the emotional roller coaster as it constantly craves these powerful substances. While an athlete and his parents are ultimately responsible for how he treats his own body, a coach, as the adult in a player-coach relationship, has a moral obligation to educate his players about what is best for his athletes.

Fundraising

Fundraising is another area that many people in athletics view from different angles. Many league presidents and school administrators operate on limited budgets and provide their teams with only the basic equipment. For example, a baseball team can usually expect to have a facility, uniforms, helmets, baseballs, and bats provided by the league or school. The coaches, players, and parents of a team have to raise the money to purchase additional items such as team jackets, team bags, and other equipment. I think fundraising is one of the most important lessons coaches can teach their players: if you want something, you should be willing to work hard for it.

I often hear coaches saying that they should have a certain top-of-the-line uniform for their team to wear or that they should have a specific piece of equipment that is the deluxe model. I will never argue with another coach who feels that his kids deserve to have the very best to succeed athletically, whether it is a particular uniform, a certain piece of equipment, or the best facilities which help players train effectively. There are too many coaches who feel adamantly that their school or league should provide whatever they want. If a coach deems an item necessary for the success of his players, and his budget does not cover it, then he and his players should be willing to work to purchase the item. The reality of coaching sports is that nearly everyone coaches on a limited budget. Leagues or schools can offer the basics, but beyond that, one should not be afraid to work to earn the funds necessary to purchase high end items that are not normally allotted for in an athletic budget.

An example of an outline for a softball league fundraiser may look like the following:

League Goal: Funds needed for uniforms/new batting cage—$10,000

Team Goal: Each of the league's 10 teams is responsible for raising $1,000.

Fundraiser: Teams will hold a "Hit-a-Thon" on the first Saturday practice of the season.

Procedure: Each player will have two weeks to enlist neighbors, family members, businesses, and others to pledge a certain cash amount, for example, 5 cents per foot. Each player will then hit 3 pitches as far as they can. Each player's longest ball will be measured by the coach and the distance in feet traveled written on each player's "Hit-a-Thon" sheet. Players then collect the donations from their sponsors. If each player can meet the individual goal of raising $100 then we will reach the league goal.

Make checks payable to: X-town Little League Softball

Funds due by: Saturday, March 15th

The key to an effort such as this one is that it has to be league-wide. Every team and player has to help out. In addition to reaching a financial goal, participating in a fundraiser teaches athletes of all ages the meaning and value of hard work. And a well-designed fundraiser places the responsibility to make improvements in the league with those that will ultimately benefit the most from them: the players. Good coaches understand that in order to run an effective athletic program they have to try to "go the extra mile" for their players, and that takes more than the basics that most leagues or schools can offer.

Facilities and Equipment

In terms of evaluating and prioritizing equipment, facilities, uniforms, and other items necessary to run your program, you have to ask yourself several questions. First, what is the most important item needed by my athletes? Second, what items would you like to improve (that you may already have in your program)? Last, what items would you like to have (that you don't have in your program already)?

My first priority for my players involves safety equipment. Every year that I have been a high school baseball coach I have ordered two new sets of catching gear, one for varsity and one for junior varsity, and a new set of team helmets. I have never been aware of an athletic director or league president who argued with a coach over the cost of purchasing new safety equipment. Replacing these items must be your top priority each year if you truly have your athletes' best interests at heart. By having certain items that you inspect at the end of a season reconditioned by a local sporting goods store, you may be able to save your school or league valuable dollars which can be used to order other items to enhance your facilities or program.

The second thing a coach needs to look at is upgrading the current facilities. Don't settle for average facilities for your athletes. You want your players to take pride in the gymnasium or the field where they spend so much time throughout the course of a season, so don't be afraid to invest time and money to improve this area. Each year that I have coached baseball, my staff and I have made improvements to some aspect of our facility. Some years the changes have been major, while in other years they have been small items. Some of these include adding: a new 8 x 18 foot scoreboard, cementing and carpeting our batting tunnel and both bullpens, adding windscreen to our outfield fence, painting our dugouts, and so on.

Depending on your sport and the age of your field or gymnasium, there are numerous ways that you can improve your facility. If you have a batting tunnel that is wearing out, raise money to buy a new one. If your dugouts need some work, buy paint and have your staff, players, or parents help give them a facelift. An indoor facility can be improved by painting the school mascot on the wall of the gymnasium. By enlisting the help of a school art teacher, you may be able to create an image or mural that will command the pride of all your staff, players, and fans. Indoor locker rooms can be enhanced by adding carpet to the floor, posters to the walls, or setting up some chairs and a television to watch game video on. Improving your facilities does not always include a major overhaul of your field or gymnasium; simply by improving one or two small areas each year you can create an exciting atmosphere that is a source of pride for you and your players.

The third way you can improve your program's standing involves looking to add new items to your current inventory. New uniforms have a way of getting today's athletes excited about an upcoming season. Ordering your school's first pitching machine is a great way to show your softball players that you are serious about getting them the offensive repetitions they need this upcoming season. A football coach may fundraise to order special uniforms for his seniors' last football game or for the big homecoming game. A basketball coach may decide that new shooting jerseys for pre-game warm ups may give his team a psychological edge that gets them keyed up each time they take the court. By adding something new to your equipment inventory or facilities, you greatly increase your chances of generating enthusiasm among your athletes for the upcoming season.

At the conclusion of each season, you and your staff should make a written list of items that you feel you need to have by the following season. Just make sure that your wish list sticks to the essentials—those things you feel are most important. My order of priorities involves safety equipment, facility upgrades, and last, new items for the upcoming season.

Running an athletic program is an important part of being a complete coach and working on improving your program will help your team to look, act, and play their best.

9

Coaches and the College Recruitment Process

It is estimated that only between 2 and 3 percent of high school athletes will participate in intercollegiate athletics.
—NCAA

Any discussion of the process of recruiting high school players for college teams should start with the incredibly low odds of athletes participating in varsity athletics at the college level. Only one in fifty high school athletes will go on to compete at the collegiate level and far fewer will receive scholarships. Coaches, players, and parents should be aware of this statistic before convincing themselves that a good high school or AAU career is a guaranteed ticket to a free or discounted education.

That being said, if an athlete has the talent, dedication, and desire to compete at the college level, then they have a right to pursue that dream. I believe the first things that should be determined are the responsibilities of the athlete, the parents, and the coach in the recruitment process. Teachers are responsible for teaching their students, while the role of the guidance counselor is to help a student through the task of applying to college. The problem with athletics is that the high school coach is paid to coach his athletes, but he is not usually trained in the area of promoting his athletes to college programs and coaches. Ultimately, it is the player's and parents' responsibility to research, contact, and visit colleges. The high school or AAU coach still can be of great assistance in this process. Before beginning the process of contacting colleges, the coach, player, and parents of the athlete would be well served by going online to the NCAA website and researching the various rules and regulations for college recruitment.

The first area where a high school coach can help a player and parents is by assessing the athlete's talent level. Most players and parents automatically assume that their son or daughter has ability; but a high school coach may be able to offer an unbiased opinion as to what level an athlete would have the best chance for success in college. This would normally lead to a discussion of the various levels of collegiate athletics.

The biggest misconception many high school athletes have is that all college athletes go to school for free. Division I colleges or universities offer a limited number of full athletic scholarships to their various athletes, while a small number of athletes are "walk-ons," which means that the school offers them no financial benefits for their efforts. Typically, the very best high school athletes who are all-state caliber may have the talent to compete at the Division I level. Division II schools offer fewer scholarships, while a greater number of athletes "walk-on" to fill out squads. Division III schools do not offer athletic scholarships. Talented high school athletes who may not have the speed or size to compete at the Division I college level often will play at Division II or III. "Walk-ons" and Division III athletes typically pay their tuition and living costs like most students by taking out loans, by working while attending school, or by getting grants or financial aid.

Once everyone involved has an understanding of the various levels of talent and scholarships available at the different collegiate levels, then it is a good idea for a coach, athlete, and parents to sit down to discuss what goals the family has regarding college. I normally start by asking the athlete and his parents the following questions:

• In which major area of study are you interested?

• Do you want to go to a big school, medium-sized school, or a small school?

• Are you considering in-state schools? Out-of-state schools? Or both?

• How far do you want to be from home?

• To schools of which athletic level (Division I, II, or III) do you want to apply?

• Have you registered with the NCAA Initial

Eligibility Clearinghouse? (This is a form one can obtain on the NCAA website or through the student's school guidance counselor which, once completed, allows NCAA colleges and universities to obtain the academic transcript of the athlete from the high school.)

Then I ask the most important question of the conversation:

• If you don't end up on the team at a particular school, would you still want to go to that school?

The reason I ask this question is that there is no way to predict whether an athlete will make the team. An athlete could decide not to play sports once he arrives at college, he may get injured, he may lose his spot on the team to future recruits, the coach who recruited him may have left the college. If the only reason an athlete is attending a particular school is for sports, I usually try to remind them that getting their education should be their primary motivation for choosing a school.

I make it clear to players and parents that it is their decision to which schools they apply, but that I may be of assistance to them in the area of athletics. If the player or parents want the high school head coach to help make a college coaching staff aware of a particular player, he may write the coaching staff a letter of recommendation, call the coaching staff to discuss the athlete's potential, or e-mail information about the athlete to that school. These contacts are often an excellent way to promote an athlete to a college coaching staff because they may be considered more objective than a player's or his parents' assessment of the athlete's talent or potential.

There are several other ways a coach can help promote an athlete to a college coaching staff. A coach may suggest certain talent showcases or camps to an athlete and his parents in an effort to have the player display his talents to a particular coaching staff or a group of scouts that may attend these events looking for potential college athletes. A word of caution regarding talent showcases: make sure that these are legitimate opportunities for athletes and that they will be attended by many colleges. If the showcases are not well run, an athlete and his parents could be wasting their time and money chasing an unrealistic scholarship dream put on by so-called "college scouts" trying to make easy money.

Another way a coach can help an athlete show his talent to college staffs is by producing a short videotape of an athlete performing fundamental skills in a particular sport. By mailing these tapes out to the schools an athlete is interested in, the high school coach helps the coaching staffs at these colleges have a better understanding of the talent the potential athlete possesses; in fact, a videotape may be more effective than a phone call

A coach who believes an athlete is talented enough to play at a higher level can be instrumental in making sure that player gets the chance. (Bob Updegrove)

or e-mail because a college coach is able to judge the athlete's talent and potential for himself.

The last suggestion that I have for any high school coach who is truly interested in helping his athletes compete at the college level is to be tenacious. One phone call or a single e-mail to a major college coach is probably not going to get the job done. Besides having responsibilities to their current players, staff, family, and university, most college coaches get bombarded with numerous e-mails, phone calls, and videotapes from eager parents and high school coaches claiming that they know of the next superstar athlete that they must hear about. If the best you can do is one letter or phone call, then you can probably assume that your athlete's name and talents will get lost in the shuffle. On the other hand, if you are willing to make a constant, consistent effort to make college coaches aware of an athlete that you truly believe has the physical and mental tools to be successful at the next level, then you greatly increase your player's chances of extending their playing career to the college level.

The college recruitment process is complex, and a coach can help a player make the best impression on college or pro scouts.

10

The Greatest Rewards

One man practicing sportsmanship is far better than fifty preaching it. —Knute Rockne

The greatest rewards of teaching and coaching young people have absolutely nothing to do with the team's record. As a young coach, I was convinced that my coaching career would be judged by the number of games and championships my teams would win over the years. This is no longer the case.

My teams still do not have the championships I envisioned, but there are certainly accomplishments that players in our baseball program have attained that would make any coach proud. Our players have earned all-district, all-region, and all-state honors. More gratifying than these players' achievements, though, is the development of the numerous athletes who have entered our program with average talent and ability levels, but who finish their careers making significant contributions to the team.

Another reward is watching some of the players you have coached compete at the next level.

Many players from our program have gone on to play baseball in college. Some of the young men I coached as student-athletes have returned to our program as coaches following their college years. As a head coach you know you have made a very positive impact on a young person's life if they want to give back to help your program once their playing days are finished. I know that the influence of my coaches remains the primary reason I entered and remain in the coaching profession.

But the most rewarding part of coaching young people is getting the opportunity to see them grow and succeed far past their playing days. I never thought that former players would call to check on how the team was doing, would e-mail me the details of their progress at college, or visit my home and school—although I did the same with my coaches after my playing days were through. I never imagined I would be speaking with former players about college courses, employment issues, and decisions in their personal lives, but being given the opportunity to listen and talk to them about life outside of sports is more important than any skill I ever taught on a basketball court or baseball field.

As an effective coach, remember that you have the opportunity to be a positive role model for young people during what can be the most enjoyable and formative periods of their lives.

Appendix

Coaching Forms and Practice Plans

The sample coaching forms cover team rules, equipment and uniform inventory, checklists for one-on-one conferences, and letters about try-outs/cuts, league budget, and fundraising activities. The practice plans cover four of the major sports offered in most schools and leagues and include plans for beginning, intermediate, and advanced athletes. Feel free to adjust them to suit your needs.

Youth League Team Rules

Little Tigers: Team Rules
- Priorities: family/religion, school, football (in that order).
- All players must attend practice.
- Show up to practice and games early. Do not be late.
- If you can't be at practice, call Coach Jones at home (555-555-5555) before practice.
- No jewelry (this is a safety issue).
- Listen to your coaches.
- Support your teammates.
- Give 100% at all times in practices and games.
- No trash talk toward opponents, fans, or coaches will be tolerated.
- Do not make negative comments to the officials.
- Practice good sportsmanship at all times.

***Breaking a team rule once will result in extra conditioning and a loss of playing time.
***Repeatedly breaking team rules will result in suspension or dismissal from the team.

I understand the team rules. By signing this, I agree to follow the rules. I understand that if I break any of the team rules that I will be responsible for accepting the consequences.

Player's signature _____

Parent's signature_____

Junior High School Basketball Player Goal Sheet

(to be hung in locker)

Team Goals:

1. Win the league championship.
2. Give up fewer than 45 points per game.
3. Beat our rival, Smalltown Junior High School.

How will you and your teammates go about attaining each team goal?

• Give 100% every day in practice and games.

• Never rest on one defensive possession all year.

• Outwork opponents, execute better, and WANT IT MORE!

Individual Goals:

1. Be our team's most outstanding leader.
2. Average over 10 rebounds per game.
3. Earn All-Conference honors.

How will you go about attaining each individual goal?

• Listen to coaches, hustle, and always stay positive.

• Assume every shot taken all year will be missed and FIGHT FOR THE BALL!

• Outplay every opponent I face in our league every night.

T-Ball/Coach Pitch Practice Plan

4:00–4:05 Jog and stretch

4:05–4:20 "Playing catch" (use tennis balls if needed)

- Teach four-seam grip, arm to the "L" position, and follow through
- Teach catching the ball with two hands

4:20–4:40 Ground ball practice

- Teach two-handed catch in proper fielding position
- Roll ground balls (10 minutes)
- Hit ground balls (10 minutes)

4:40–5:00 Hitting practice / outfield practice

- 6 players in each group
- Hitting – 3 groups of two
- Rotate 5 swings each, hitting tennis balls off T (toward the fence)
- Teach players to keep eyes on the ball throughout the swing
- Outfield – All six players in one group / one line
- Players rotate catching fly ball (use tennis ball) thrown by coach
- Teach players to catch ball with two hands above their head

5:00–5:30 Scrimmage situation

Offense

- Teach players to hit with eyes on the ball
- Teach base runners to listen to their coaches

Defense
- Teach players to catch ball with two hands
- Teach players to throw ball to lead base to get an out

Reminders
- Team Picture is Saturday at 9:30 AM
- Practice is Saturday from 10 AM–11:30 AM

AAU/Junior High Baseball Practice Plan

4:00–4:20 Warmup
- Run and stretch (10 minutes)
- Long toss (10 minutes)

4:20–4:30 Defensive position practice
- OFs in outfield, middle IFs at 2B, corner IFs at 1st/3rd, catchers behind home plate area (10 minutes)

4:30–5:00 Team defense
- Live situations – coach hits each repetition to make sure every position gets defensive repetitions (10 minutes)
- 1st and 3rd situations (10 minutes)
- Flyball communication – coaches throw fly balls in short RF, short CF, short LF and in foul ground to force player communication on every repetition – "I got it!" (10 minutes)

5:00–5:30 Pitchers – bullpen
Batting practice
- (1 bunt, 1 hit-and-run, 8 swings per batter)

5:30–5:50 Base running
- H to 1st, 1st to 3rd, delay steal, reading dirt balls

5:50–5:55 Drag bunt contest
• Losers pick up the balls
5:55–6:00 Rake and drag baselines, infield,
pitcher's mound, etc.

High School Baseball Practice Plan

3:40–3:50 Jog / stretch
3:50–4:00 Long toss
• 2 minutes each distance – 30 ft., 60 ft., 90 ft.,
120 ft., 30 ft. (both players run to trade places
on any unsuccessful throw/catch)
4:00–4:10 Defensive position practice (OF, middle IF, corner IF, catchers)
4:10–4:20 Live defensive repetitions
• Coach A hits to IF – plays at 1B, double plays
at 2B, and plays at home plate with infielders
positioned in the infield grass
• Coach B hits to OF – all throws must hit cut
off man
4:20–5:00 Pitchers – bullpen (drills + 10 fast-
balls, 10 change ups, 10 curve balls, 20 alternate)
Varsity batting practice on field – 2 bunts, 8
swings (+ T drills / soft toss)
Junior Varsity BP in batting tunnel – 2 bunts,
8 swings (+ T drills / soft toss)
5:00–5:20 Team defense
• Pick offs – 2 lines of pitchers on mound –
pitchers alternate between lines picking off
runners at 1B and 2B (10 minutes)
• Rundowns – 2 rundowns: 1B and 2B / 2B and
3B – starts with pick off from P (10 minutes)

5:20–5:35 Base running
  • Home to 1st, stealing 2nd, tagging up at 3rd
5:35–5:40 Squeeze bunt contest
  • Each position on the team chooses their best bunter (winning team skips field clean up today)
5:40–5:45 Clean up the field
Reminders
  • Bus leaves for tomorrow's game at 4 PM
  • Be ready for the bus at 3:45

Youth League Basketball Practice Plan

4:00–4:05 Jog 3 laps + stretch

4:05–4:15 Full-court dribbling drills

• Teach / stress keeping eyes up while dribbling

  A. Speed dribble

  B. Stop-and-Go dribble

  C. Spin dribble

4:15–4:25 Passing drills

• Teach / stress passing the ball to target or teammate's chest

  A. Chest pass

  B. Bounce pass

  C. Overhead pass

4:25–4:35 Lay-ups

• Teach proper footwork and angle from the wing

• Practice lay-ups from both sides using two lines

4:35–4:50 Shooting drills

• Teach / stress "B-E-E-F" = Balance (with knees bent), Eyes (on the rim), Elbow (tucked beneath the ball), and Follow through (5 minutes)

• Two minutes at each spot (5 to 10 feet) – left baseline, left wing, center of the lane, right wing, right baseline (10 minutes)

4:50–5:15 Defensive footwork drills

• Players slide sideways and backward following coach pointing directionally – teach players not to cross their feet (10 minutes)

- Players slide sideways and backwards reacting to coach dribbling – stress not crossing their feet (10 minutes)
- Player guards dribbler one-on-one full court sliding feet reacting to the dribbler (5 minutes)

5:15–5:30 Scrimmage
- Stress / teach – taking good shots on offense
- Guarding your man on defense

Reminders
- Game on Saturday is 2 PM; be here by 1:45

AAU Basketball Practice Plan

4:00–4:05 5 laps + stretch

4:05–4:15 3-on-2 / 2-on-1 full-court drill
- Stress: "Always get a good shot!"

4:15–4:25 Rebounding drill
- 3 rebounds to get out (3 players compete to see who gets 3 rebounds first)

4:25–4:35 Kentucky Drill
- 4 vs 4 vs 4 half-court scrimmage – winning team stays on the court on offense; losing team goes out; team that comes on next starts out on defense

4:35–4:45 Guard drills / post player drills
- Guards practice dribbling / passing to the post / perimeter shooting
- Post players practice interior screens and post moves near basket

4:45–4:55 Offensive plays (with no defense)
- Point guard calls play; team executes each play; make sure substitutes get repetitions

4:55–5:10 Defense
- One-on-one full court – defender vs dribbler (5 minutes)
  - Teach / stress – defender staying low and not crossing feet
  - Defending the pass to the wing (10 minutes)
  - Teach / stress – defender must keep a hand in the passing lane

5:10–5:30 Scrimmage
- Man-to-man full-court press (10 minutes)
- Both teams play 2-3 half-court zone defense (10 minutes)
  - Stress / teach – importance of working as a team on offense; communicate and be aggressive on defense

Reminders
- Practice tomorrow at 4 PM

High School Basketball Practice Plan

4:00–4:05 Jog / stretch

4:05–4:10 Triangle passing (groups of three)
- Drill stresses passing both directions – bounce pass, over the defender pass, dribble sideways and then pass

4:10–4:15 Full court offense drills (in pairs)
- Pass back and forth length of court + lay-up
- Pass back and forth – jump shot on the wing
- Pass back and forth – jump shot at foul line

4:15–4:25 6 stations x 90 seconds each
   A. Dribbling drills
   B. 3-step lay-ups

C. Mikan drill

D. Drop step shots

E. Elbow jumpers

F. 1-on-1 moves

4:25–4:30 10 foul shots

- Shoot w/ partner
- Use all 6 baskets

4:30–4:40 Guard / post player series (in pairs)

- Use all 6 baskets
- Guard series (5 moves) – lay-up to right, jumper to right, lay-up to left, jumper to left, jumper
- Post series (3 moves) – drop step lay-up, turn around to the middle jump shot, up-and-under pump fake to lay-up

4:40–5:20 Defense

A. 1-on-1 full court

B. Defending the wing – stress hand in passing lane

C. Shell drill – emphasize helping out on weak side – "See the ball while you are on the weak side!"

5:20–5:25 10 foul shots

- 2 shots each to 10
- Shoot w/ partner
- Use all 6 baskets

5:25–5:35 Scrimmage – full-court man-to-man defense (both teams)

5:35–5:40 10 foul shots

- 5 each to 10
- Shoot w/ partner

- Use all 6 baskets

5:40–5:50 Scrimmage – half-court zone 1-3-1 zone trap (both teams)

5:50–5:55 Review sidelines inbounds play / review scoring inbounds plays

5:55–6:00 Pressure free throws / conditioning
- Make 2 of 2 = no running, make 1 of 2 = 1 sprint, miss both = 2 sprints

Reminders
- Practice tomorrow from 4 PM–6 PM

PeeWee Soccer Practice Plan

8:00–8:10 Jog a lap / stretch

8:10–8:20 Dribbling drills
- Speed dribble (to midfield and back)
- Change directions (using cones – to midfield and back)

8:20–8:35 Passing
- 1 Line – to stationary coach (5 minutes)
- Pairs – 2 players are ten feet apart (5 minutes)
- Triangle (formation) passing – change directions on the whistle (5 minutes)

8:35–8:50 Throw ins
- Teach rule: feet on ground
- Teach technique: two hands + ball behind head + follow through (5 minutes)
- 1 Line – to stationary target / coach (5 minutes)
- Pairs – back and forth with partner 10 feet away (5 minutes)

8:50–9:10 Goal and corner kicks
- Goal kicks – offensive and defensive alignments (10 minutes)
- Corner kicks – offensive and defensive alignments (10 minutes)

9:10–9:30 Scrimmage – half field
- Four players vs two coaches (10 minutes) + four players vs four players (10 minutes)
- Teach / emphasize: Spreading out / don't bunch together and passing to open teammates

Reminder
- Practice is next Saturday at 8 AM

Select/Travel Soccer Team Practice Plan

10:00–10:10 Jog / stretch

10:10–10:25 Dribbling drills (both feet)
- Speed dribble – length of field, L/R
(5 minutes)
- Change direction – length of field, zig-zag
(5 minutes)
- Change speed / stop and go – to midfield, L/R
(5 minutes)

10:25–10:50 Passing drills (both feet)
- Pairs – 10 to 20 feet apart (5 minutes)
- Triangle – 20 feet apart / both directions
(5 minutes)
- "Pairs on the move" – Pair runs field exchanging passes with teammate (10 minutes)
- 3-on-1 passing – "keep away" from the defender (5 minutes)

10:50–11:00 Throw ins – emphasize feet on ground + proper technique
- Pairs – 25 feet apart – to stationary partner
(5 minutes)
- Pairs – 15 to 25 feet apart – to a moving partner (5 minutes)

11:00–11:10 Corner kicks
- Offense – set play
- Defense – guarding opponents

11:10–11:20 Goal kicks – placing kick to teammates to retain possession

11:20–11:35 Scrimmage – half field

11:35–11:50 Scrimmage – full field

11:50–Noon Penalty kicks
- Two squads – shoot while you're tired to simulate overtime penalty kicks that may determine the outcome of a game – losers shag balls.

Reminder
- Practice is Monday from 4 PM to 6 PM

High School/Advanced Travel Soccer Practice Plan

Noon–12:15 Jog + stretch + agility drills
12:15–12:30 Dribbling drills – both feet
- Speed dribble / change of direction / stop-and-go (length of field)
- Live 1-on-1 vs defender (to midfield)
12:30–12:55 Passing drills – both feet
- Pair + triangle – 25 to 30 feet apart
(5 minutes)
- 2-on-1 passing drill – "keep away" from the defender (5 minutes)
- Triangle passing drill – 3-on-2 "keep away"
(5 minutes)
- To a moving "guarded" teammate
(10 minutes)
12:55–1:05 Throw ins
- 30 to 60 feet to a moving target
1:05–1:25 Corner kicks
- Offense – set play to teammate moving toward ball / goal
- Defense – identifying / staying with offensive players

1:25–1:50 Scrimmage – full length of field

1:50–2:00 Penalty kicks – losers shag balls and complete extra conditioning

Reminder

- First game of tournament is this Saturday at 10 AM. ***Be at field by 9:30 AM.

PeeWee Football Practice Plan

4:00–4:05 Jog to get loose / stretch

4:05–4:15 Agility drills (zig-zag drills, lateral movements, follow the ball)

4:15–4:25 Form tackling drill – teach / stress keeping head up (to prevent neck injuries) and wrapping up / using two arms to tackle

4:25–4:40 Offensive position drills
  • Quarterback / running back – hand off and pitch to running back
  • Linemen – blocking scheme vs no defense / or coach on defense
  • Wide receivers – five yard, turn and catch + blocking your defender

4:40–4:55 Defensive position drills
  • Linemen – attacking gaps vs coaches as offensive linemen
  • Linebackers – working in same drill – reading and reacting to the ball / coach
  • Defensive backs / safety – backpedaling + breaking / reacting to ball

4:55–5:10 Scrimmage
  • Offense vs defense – 10 plays (huddle with coach after each play)
  • Any play that gains 3 yards or more = 1 point for offense
  • Any play the defense stops before 3 yards = 1 point for defense
  • Team that gets most points out of 10 plays wins the drill

5:10–5:25 Special teams
- Punt coverage – stress / teach – staying in your lanes
- Punt return – stress / teach – situations to return or fair catch

5:25–5:30 Conditioning – sit-ups, push-ups, 10-yard sprint (3x)

Reminders
- Game Saturday is at 8 AM – Be at the field no later than 7:30

Junior High Football Practice Plan

4:00–4:05 Jog a lap around the field / stretch

4:05–4:10 Agilities – lateral step drill, front-back shuffle, read and react drill

4:10–4:15 Form running – stress explosive first step

A. From 3-point stance – 10 yards
B. From athletic stance – 10 yards
C. 20-yard sprint (3x)

4:15–4:25 Form tackling drill – stress head up (for safety) and wrap using two arms

4:25–4:55 Offensive position drills
- QBs / running backs – handoffs, pitches, screen passes in the flat
- Linemen – blocking schemes – pulling, trap block + pass blocking
- Wide receivers – slant routes + out routes + blocking cornerback

4:55–5:20 Defensive position drills

- Linemen + linebackers – reading and reacting to run plays – blitzing / defending the pass
- Secondary – quick feet drills, backpedaling + breaking on the ball, defending the slant route, "prevent" coverage = no deep passes

5:20–5:45 Scrimmage situations
- 5 plays – 1st and 10 yards to go
- 5 plays – 2nd and 5 yards to go
- 5 plays – 3rd and short (2 yards or less)
- 5 plays – Goal line plays or 2-point conversion plays

5:45–5:55 Special teams
- Kick off coverage – stay in lanes + sprint to the ball
- Kick off return – front line = watch the kick for onside kick – return men = catch + get to the wall of blockers

5:55–6:00 Conditioning – push-ups, sit-ups, up-down drill, 20-yard sprints

Reminder
- Team meal tomorrow after practice in cafeteria

High School Football Practice Plan

4:00–4:05 Jog a lap / stretch

4:05–4:15 Agility drills – lateral strides, front-back shuffle, first step drill

4:15–4:25 Form tackling drill – head up (for safety) and wrap with two arms

4:25–4:45 Offensive position drills
- QBs / running backs – handoffs, pitches, screens, play action fake

- Linemen – pull, trap, goal line, pass protect, screen blocking
- Wide receivers – slant out, hitch-and-go, up-and-out, fly pattern

4:45–5:05 Defensive position drills
- Linemen – attacking gaps, run blitz, pass blitz, stunt
- Inside LB – reading RB / guard vs run, covering middle pass
- Outside LB – containing the run, covering pass to the outside / flat
- Secondary – footwork drills, break on the out, break on the slant, zone coverages, prevent coverage = keep receivers in front of you

5:05–5:35 Scrimmage series
- 5 plays – 1st and 10 yards to go
- 5 plays – 2nd and 7 yards to go
- 5 plays – 3rd and 7 yards to go
- 5 plays – 3rd and short (2 yards or less)
- 5 plays – Goal line series / 2-point conversions

5:35–5:45 Punt coverage / kick off coverage – stress staying in your lanes

5:45–5:55 Fake punt / onside kick – not used often, but very important!

5:55–6:00 Conditioning – sit-ups, push-ups, up-downs, 10- / 20- / 40-yard sprints

Reminders
- Game tomorrow at 6 PM; be in locker room by 4:45 for pre-game

Youth League Softball Preseason One-on-One Conference Checklist

City Prep Softball

Player's Name: _____

Coach asks, "How do you think the team is doing so far?"

"I think we look pretty good. We should win a lot of games this year."

Coach asks, "How would you rate your own performance so far?"

"OK on defense. I need to practice more on my hitting."

Coach lists player's strengths:

"I think your arm strength will help us on defense, and your speed on the bases will be a big positive on offense."

Coach lists areas player needs to improve:

"I noticed you have been struggling with backhand ground balls. We will improve this skill by throwing and hitting repetitions to your backhand every day in practice."

Coach describes player's role at this point:

"Right now, I think you have a chance to get innings at second base. Whether you are a starter or a reserve player depends on how the rest of our practices and scrimmages go during the remainder of the preseason. Keep working hard."

Checklist for High School Football One-on-One Postseason Conference

Big Park High School Football

Player's Name: _____

Collect uniform (helmet, pads, jersey, pants, belt, socks).

1. "How do you think the team did this year?"

2. "How would you rate your overall, individual performance this season?"

3. "What were your positive individual accomplishments this season?"

4. "What areas do you feel you could have had more success in?"

5. "What camps, clinics, or leagues are you participating in this off season?"

6. Give camp brochures, league information, and weight lifting program to player.

7. Give end of season banquet information to player.

8. Stress importance of off-season classroom commitment.

9. "Thanks for all your hard work. I appreciate your efforts."

High School Baseball Equipment Inventory

Equipment	# of pieces	Condition
Baseballs	10 doz.	Fair
Bats	6	Fair
Catcher's Gear	2	Good
Helmets	8	Good
Batting Tees	5	Bad
Plastic Balls	50	Fair
Tennis Balls	50	Good
BP Screen	1	Bad
Bases	Full set	Fair
Water Cooler	1	Good
Scorebook	1	Good

Other comments:

Athletic Director,

Most items listed on my inventory will last another year, but the items I described as "bad" need to be replaced before the upcoming season. Also, could we get a few dozen new baseballs for games? The "fair" baseballs from last year will be okay for practice, but I would like new baseballs for game night.

Thanks for helping supply us with what we need.

Coach Adams

High School Uniform Inventory

Team: Varsity Basketball

Jersey #	Jersey Size
10	Small
11	Small
15	Small
21	Small
25	Medium
30	Medium
31	Medium
20	Medium
40	Medium
41	Large
42	Large
45	Large
50	Large

Pants sizes	# of Pairs
Small	4
Medium	5
Large	4

Other Comments:

Athletic Director,

I will pass last year's varsity uniforms down to the junior varsity. We will pass their uniforms down to the freshmen team. What do you want me to do with last year's freshmen team uniforms? Should I use them for practice gear? Donate them to the local Little League?

Coach Lewis

Letters Regarding Tryouts/Cuts

Date:_____

Dear _____,

I want to take the time to thank you for your interest in the Smallville Junior High School (SJHS) Football team. As you know, tryouts involve a week of drills and scrimmage situations that allow each athlete to showcase their talents.

As we informed all athletes trying out at the preseason meeting and on day one of tryouts, the criteria for making the team include: outstanding athletic ability in terms of size, speed, and strength, football talent demonstrated through blocking and tackling drills, and intangible qualities like always hustling, having a good attitude, and displaying good sportsmanship.

Coach Edmonson
SJHS Football Coach

(If athlete made team)

Dear _____,

I am pleased to inform you that you are one of the 35 athletes that have earned the privilege to be on this year's team. Practice will begin with a review of team rules on the practice field at 3:45 tomorrow. Be ready to work hard!

OR

(If athlete is cut)

Dear _____,

Unfortunately, I can not keep everyone on the team who tries out each season. I feel that there are students who are more advanced athletically than you at this time so I regret to inform you that you did not make this year's team. Continue to train hard, and I encourage you to come out for the team again next year. Thanks for your time and effort.

Sincerely,

Coach Edmonson
SJHS Football Coach

Youth League Projected Budget Letter to Parents

Dear Parents,

I am including the following budget so everyone is aware of how their $100 registration fee is being used for the upcoming season.

Coach Wilson

Budget allowance: 15 players x $100 = $1,500

Expenditure	Cost	Description/Explanation
Umpires	$500	2 umpires per game x 10 games x $25 per game
Baseballs	$100	8 dozen x $12.50 per doz.
Helmets	$100	4 helmets x $25 each
Catcher's gear	$200	2 sets x $100 per set
Batting tees	$125	5 tees x $25 per tee
Water cooler	$35	1 cooler at $35
Scorebook	$20	1 scorebook at $20
Snacks	$100	Gatorade, oranges, etc.
Trophies	$120	15 end-of-year trophies x $8 per trophy
Party	$200	End-of-year pizza party (includes 10 pizzas, unlimited soda, and dessert)
TOTAL	$1,500	

Total funds remaining at season's conclusion $0

Youth League Fundraising Letters

2005 Cubs Little League Fundraiser

Dear _____,

The members of the 2005 Cubs Little League baseball team need your help. Unfortunately, the Township Little League can not afford all the equipment needed for our upcoming season, so we are asking you or your business to support our efforts.

Our goal is to buy three bats and five new helmets for the upcoming season. To defray the cost of these items we are selling beach towels to citizens and businesses in the Township limits.

The cost for one towel is $15 or $25 for two towels. The towels are 2 feet wide by 6 feet long. You may choose from either red or blue towels.

Thank you for your support of Township Little League Baseball. We hope you can make it to the ballpark this season.

Please check one of the following:

_____ 1 Red towel = $15
_____ 1 Blue towel = $15
_____ 2 Red towels = $25
_____ 2 Blue towels= $25
_____ 1 Red + 1 Blue towel = $25

Name: _____

Phone: _____

Address: _____

_____

Please make checks payable to: Township Little League and mail with this form to the address below.

Thanks again for your support. If you have any questions about this fundraiser you may call me at home at (555) 555-5555.

Doug Smith
Cubs Coach
Township Little League
P.O. Box 3
Anytown, IL 60000

First Annual Southern High School Basketball Shoot-A-Thon

The Southern High School Basketball team needs your help!!! In order to raise funds to buy new uniforms for next year's team, the Southern High School Basketball team is holding its first annual Shoot-A-Thon!

During this Saturday's practice, each player will shoot 100 free throws. We are asking businesses and citizens like you to support the Southern High School basketball team's effort to purchase new uniforms by pledging a donation to a player on this year's team. Donations may be made in the amount of a flat donation or by each free throw made out of 100 (for example, $0.10 per made shot x 70 made shots = $7 donation).

All shooters will be supervised throughout the Shoot-A-Thon by a member of the basketball coaching staff. All donations are gratefully accepted. Please make checks payable to: Southern High School Basketball Booster Club. Thank you for supporting the team and we hope to see you at a game this season.

Coach Walsh
SHS Basketball Coach

Player's Name: Jeffrey Shooter
Number of shots made: _____ / 100
Supporter's Name   Donation ($)   Phone

1.
2.
3.

(numbered list of supporters continues)

Jones Youth Soccer Association Fundraiser

50/50 Raffle

The 30 teams of the Jones Youth Soccer Association are selling 50/50 raffle tickets to raise money to defer costs for uniforms, field maintenance, and referees for the upcoming season. Each player in the league is being asked to sell five 50/50 Raffle tickets.

The cost of each ticket is $5. If each player in the league sells $25 in raffle tickets, more than $10,000 dollars will be raised. That means that the winner of the raffle will win over $5,000!!! The other $5,000 will go to the Jones Youth Soccer Association to buy new equipment, maintain the fields, and defray costs for transportation to away games.

The 50/50 drawing will take place at 8 AM at the Jones Soccer Field on opening day of the season (fill in date). You do not need to be present at the drawing to win. Just make sure you fill out both copies of the raffle ticket with your contact information so we can let you know if you're the lucky winner. Please make checks payable to: Jones Youth Soccer Association. Good luck and thanks for your support of the Jones Youth Soccer Association!

J. Jones
JYSA President

Supporter's Copy: Ticket #158

League Copy (to be placed in raffle)
Ticket #158
Name: _____
Phone: _____
Address: _____
_____
_____

Erieville Junior High School Football Fundraiser

Firewood Sale

Dear Erieville Junior High School Football Fans,

Members of the EJHS Football team are selling firewood in an effort to raise funds needed for new equipment in our school weight room. Using money from the firewood sale, we hope to purchase: three new bench presses, two new curl bars, and two new squat racks.

It is a win-win proposition. By purchasing a truckload of firewood, you'll be supporting our players' efforts to improve their results on the football field, while saving yourself the time and energy it takes to cut, load, and stack your own firewood. That's right—We'll deliver the wood to your house and we'll stack it for you!!!

The cost for a truckload of wood is $75. We will make all deliveries on [DATE] between 8 AM and Noon. Please try to be home during this time so you can tell us where you want us to stack the wood. Also, please make sure you have cleared a dry area ahead of time so we can make all deliveries in a timely manner.

Thanks for supporting our players and please feel free to contact me at the school if you have any questions regarding this or any of our other fundraisers.

Coach Gregory
EJHS Football Coach

Name: _____

Phone: _____

Address: _____

_____

_____

Please make check for $75 to: Erieville Junior High School Football Team.

I **will** / **will not** be home on [DATE] between 8 AM and Noon.

If I am not home when you deliver the wood, please stack the wood (please indicate a location below):

_____

Acknowledgements

I wish to thank the following people who influenced me through my career as a player, coach, and writer.

The Cassidy and Wiley families who have supported me as an athlete, coach, son, brother, and in-law.

Steve Welpott who made sure I learned two things in Little League baseball: how to play the game and how to have fun. He taught me that a great coach gets his players to become better without realizing they are working at it.

Wayne Todd taught me the positive uses of organization, practice planning, and discipline when leading an athletic team. It is not by accident that these are the same qualities that are my strength as a coach. The numerous late night phone calls over the last decade have taught me more about coaching than any clinic or video.

OJ Lamp made sure that high school baseball was about more than the game on the field, and helped me out when it came time for me to coach high school pitchers. His system of teaching pitchers remains the basis for every pitcher I work with today.

Mike Lonergan showed me that age is no factor in being a quality coach and illustrated the numerous ways to improve a program—running camps, scheduling tough competition, and traveling among them. His determination to take a small college basketball program and have it ranked nationally, year in and year out, proved to me what one coach's vision can do for an entire athletic program.

Joe Cochran and Larry Boomer served as examples for how I should always conduct myself when coaching young people—with class and like a gentleman.

John Costello explained to me that coaching is not about the coaches; it is about the players. Getting me to remember "It ain't about you!" in the numerous difficult situations all coaches face in practices and games has made me a much better coach. His advice over the years, both personally and professionally, has been invaluable.

Jason Bagby was there for me when I was twenty-two years old and a newly named head coach. The only thing better than playing Little League and high school baseball together was coaching with him at Broad Run. His systems for teaching infielders and hitters remain the basis for how I teach players now, a decade after we started.

Brett Lewis picked up where Jason Bagby left off. To lose one right hand man I trusted and leaned on and gain another shows how lucky I have been as a coach. Brett's support for me as a coach will not be forgotten.

Matt Wiley put up with me when I coached him, when we coached together, and let me marry his sister. He taught me that a coach can make his best player better and it is common sense to hit your best hitter in the lead-off position. As family, I have always thought of him as a brother. I appreciate everything he's done for me on the field and off.

Jeffrey "Colt" Fletcher and Chris Null came back to coach the players in the same program we were a part of ourselves. Nothing is more gratifying than watching the two of them work with players in our program.

Kevin Weeren and Jeff Hawes showed me the dedication it takes to run a year-round program. By letting me get a look inside their basketball programs, they gave me a better understanding of the methods I can use to improve my own program: overnight trips, fundraising, summer camps, summer leagues, clinics for my feeder programs, and so on. By allowing me to understand and use some of their ideas, they both helped me to create a more positive, well-rounded experience for the players in my program.

My publisher, Bruce H. Franklin, took a chance on an unknown writer and his manuscript. He provided advice and guidance on how to take what was essentially my personal experience as a coach and form it into a set of guidelines and tips that could be useful to other coaches.

Noreen O'Connor and Sue Anne Cassidy helped shape the manuscript and painstakingly read through my various drafts. Their attention to detail and numerous ideas have improved the final book.

Bob Updegrove, Beth Pearson, and the Broad Run High School Yearbook staff captured coaches and athletes in action through their photographs. Their snapshots offer readers a true look at coaches at work.